Hyp
Spirituality

Hypnotic Spirituality

Harnessing the power of hypnosis
to accelerate your spiritual growth

Philippe Pascal

Copyright © 2013 by Philippe Pascal

All rights reserved. No part of the book may be reproduced by any mechanical, photographic, or electronic process or in the form of phonographic recording; nor may it be stored in a retrieval system, transmitted, or otherwise be copied for public or private use – other than for "fair use" as brief quotations – without prior written permission of the author.

The author of this book is not a medical doctor and does not dispense medical advice or prescribe the use of any technique as a form of treatment for physical, emotional, or medical problems without the advice of a physician directly or indirectly. The intent of the author is only to offer information of a general nature to help you in your quest for emotional and spiritual well-being. In the event you use any of the information in this book for yourself, which is your constitutional right, the author and the publisher assume no responsibility for your actions.

ISBN: 978-1475291315

Acknowledgement

I want to thank my wife Julie for her contribution to this book. Her extensive hypnotherapy experience, deep understanding of the Course and ongoing support have been instrumental in making this book possible.

CONTENTS

Preface i

Introduction iii

    Who is this book for? iv

    Getting the most benefit from this book iv

    Structure.. vi

    Important Note viii

Part 1 - Introduction To A Course in Miracles 1

Chapter One - Overview of A Course in Miracles 3

    How the Course came about 4

    Intent 5

    Terminology 5

    Central message 8

    How did we (appear to) get here? 9

    Levels 12

    Metaphorical language...13

Chapter Two - Right or Wrong 15

    Wrong-mindedness: the ego thought system 15

    Projection and the cycle of guilt.............................16

    Special relationships...18

    Right-Mindedness - The Holy Spirit's thought system 19

Chapter Three - Key Concepts 23

    A Call for love 23

    Miracles 24

    Living in peace 26

    Summary of key principles 27

    Quotation references 30

Part 2 - Overview of Hypnosis and Hypnotherapy 31

Introduction 33

Chapter Four - Brief History 35

Chapter Five - Introduction to Hypnotherapy 41

An occult art or a natural phenomenon? 41

Definition 42

What does it feel like? 42

What is it good for? 43

The power of the subconscious 44

How is hypnotherapy different from conventional therapy? 47

Conscious Critical Faculty 47

Selective thinking 49

Levels of trance 49

The role of the therapist 52

Chapter Six - Hypnosis Myths Debunked 55

Chapter Seven - Methods of Hypnotherapy 63

Suggestion therapy 63

Positive suggestions 63

Metaphors 65

Analytical therapy 67

Parts Therapy 67

Regression therapy 68

Time-track therapy 71

Non-directed regression therapy 72

Past Life Regression 74

Chapter Eight - A Guide to Self-Hypnosis 79

Structure 79

How to write good suggestion scripts 80

Use of metaphors 82

Your self-hypnosis session 83

Part 3 - Hypnotic Spirituality 85

Introduction.. 87
Chapter Nine - Ain't No Sacrifice... At All 89
  Have an honest look at it..90
  A glimpse of Home 97
  Time Warp 100
Chapter Ten - Back to School! 103
  Welcome to your new school...............................104
  A custom curriculum 104
  A self-paced course 106
  Social interaction 107
  When do I graduate?...109
  In practice 110
Chapter Eleven - Just an Illusion................................. 113
  How it all started 113
  Projection 114
  The time of my life 117
  The ultimate repressed thought............................123
  People say I'm a dreamer... and I *am* the only one 126
  The best screen ever 129
  Hierarchy of illusions 131
  Body of evidence 135
Chapter Twelve - Face Lift...................................... 139
  The blame game 140
  Taking responsibility 142
  In practice 144
Chapter Thirteen - The ~~Devil~~ Ego Made Me Do It......... 149
  The new satan 150
  Das Gestalt 155
  Resistance..156
  Ego weakening 158
  You're so special...160
  The ego strikes back 161

Chapter Fourteen - A Part of Me......................................**165**
Parts therapy...166
Billions of parts...169
Your own parts therapy 169
In Practice...171

Chapter Fifteen - I've Got the Power! **175**
A split mind is a terrible thing 176
The choice is yours 177
Decisions, decisions, decisions…. 181
What's your problem? 183
The right way to ask 185
I hope I am wrong 188
Be careful what you wish for..190

Chapter Sixteen - Whose Life Is It Anyway?.................**193**
It's my life..194
Thanks for the memory...197
A therapy of many lifetimes 200
Identity crisis 201

Chapter Seventeen - Just Undo It! **203**
Make it a habit 204
Say that one more time! 206
Keep it real 208
The sound of silence 211
Clearing the field 213

Chapter Eighteen - A New Prophet **215**
Prophet or Teacher? 215
A call for love...218
In practice..220

Conclusion **225**

Appendix A - Sample Scripts **229**

Sample Induction 230

Sample Deepener 234

Sample Emerging Script 236

Appendix B - Resources **237**

Recommended Reading 239

Recommended movies 241

Hypnotherapy web sites 241

PREFACE

Are you following a spiritual path but find it hard to apply its principles consistently, even though you understand them intellectually? Do you feel your spiritual growth is painfully slow and wonder if you are actually making any progress at all, no matter how much you study? Have you noticed how, as soon as you seem to make a little spiritual progress and feel a bit more at peace, you appear to fall back into old habits. Do you wish there were a way to make these spiritual habits "stick"?

If so, you are not alone. More and more people are following a spiritual path nowadays. Many have been disillusioned with the rhetoric, rigidity and rituality of organized religions and have turned to less conventional forms of spirituality. And it seems that, regardless of the approach taken, we all struggle to apply the principles we learn, and the spiritual progress we make comes at a snail's pace.

This book aims to facilitate and accelerate the application of the principles of the spiritual path you are following by utilizing the power of hypnosis and hypnotherapy. Hypnosis excels at "reprogramming" the mind, enabling the breaking of bad habits and the adoption of new ones quickly and safely. It has been

Preface

used to help people solve countless issues from fears and phobias to nail biting to weight problems to improving their golf swing.

In this book, you will learn how to harness the power of your subconscious mind by using hypnosis techniques to more easily follow the ways of the particular spiritual path you have chosen.

INTRODUCTION

There are many spiritual paths. Some paths are more direct, and therefore faster than others, but all are equally valid and all eventually lead (back) to the same place: perfect Oneness with our Source. The sages in history all had essentially the same message at the core of their teaching. The mythology (i.e. the stories and legends that metaphorically convey the message) and the terminology they used varied, but the content was pretty consistent. Unfortunately, this message has often been misunderstood, distorted over time and wrapped in layers of rituals, to the point where it is hard to see clearly the essence of the message.

My personal spiritual path follows the teachings of *A Course in Miracles*, a drastically different spiritual approach based on forgiveness and non-dualism (i.e. there is God and nothing else; human life and the world we perceive are an illusion). Therefore, this book will refer to *A Course in Miracles* and its teachings, and describe how hypnotherapy can be applied to help follow its principles. However, this, in no way, prevents you from adapting the techniques to any other spiritual approach.

Introduction

WHO IS THIS BOOK FOR?

If you are *A Course in Miracles* student, and despite understanding the philosophy and the principles at an intellectual level, you still struggle to apply them, this book is for you. If you feel like your spiritual progress is painfully slow, or even experience what seems like negative progress (i.e. you thought you got past some issue and realize that you're worse off now than you used to be), then this book can help you.

If you are a hypnotherapist and want practical methods to help your clients with their spiritual growth, the techniques listed in part 3 will prove useful. Be sure to read part 1 if you are not familiar with *A Course in Miracles*; otherwise the techniques will not make sense.

However, if you're looking for a way to "bypass the system" and are hoping that, by reading this book, you can get away with not studying the Course or doing the lessons in the Workbook, then put this book back on the shelf. This book is definitively a *complement* to the Course, not a substitute. It is merely an aid in applying its principles throughout your day and in living a more peaceful, loving, forgiving life with the eventual goal to return to your true Self.

GETTING THE MOST BENEFIT FROM THIS BOOK

This book details how hypnotherapeutic techniques can be used to help speed up your spiritual progress. You will learn a variety of methods designed to help you apply the Course's principles to your everyday life, in a way that is automatic and unconscious.

To get the most benefit from the techniques, you would ideally seek an experienced hypnotherapist to take you through the hypnosis process. A good therapist will help you get into the deep state of hypnosis required to apply the techniques, and can work with you on applying the methods described in this book. However, I recommend selecting a therapist who is also a *Course in Miracles* student, or has at least an interest in this spiritual path. If your therapist thinks *A Course in Miracles* is heresy or absurd, he is unlikely to be very helpful. So, choose your therapist wisely. Explain clearly to any potential therapist what you are trying to achieve, and do not hesitate to enquire as to their own spiritual inclination.

Note that the term "hypnotherapist" has a different meaning depending on location. In some places, this term can only legally be used by people who are medical doctors or psychologists. In these locales, the word "hypnotist" must be used by hypnosis practitioners who are not medical doctors. In this book, I will use the general word "hypnotherapist" to designate a professional practitioner (whether medical doctor or lay practitioner) who uses hypnosis techniques. If you live in a jurisdiction where the use of the term "hypnotherapist" is restricted, and are looking for someone to help you with your "hypnotic spirituality" (including applying the techniques taught here), make sure you search for "hypnotists" and not just "hypnotherapists" as there's no need to limit yourself to medical doctors.

If you cannot find a hypnotherapist in your area who is also *A Course in Miracles* student, or appreciates its teachings, you may be able to get a remote session organized with such a therapist. Sessions can be

Introduction

conducted via phone or Skype; so, it is definitely an option if you have no suitable therapist locally and can't travel to visit one.

Another good option is to listen to recordings of hypnosis sessions. To that effect, I have recorded a series of sessions matching the material covered in this book. These are available from my web site: www.hypnoticspirituality.com

Finally, you can create your own self-hypnosis recordings. In Chapter 8, I will teach you how to practice self-hypnosis and how to write your own self-hypnosis scripts.

STRUCTURE

Part 1 offers an overview of *A Course in Miracles*. This section does not claim to be a comprehensive guide, but rather an introduction to the key concepts necessary to understand the subsequent sections of the book. Of course, I highly recommend reading *A Course in Miracles* and working through its 365 daily workbook lessons. I also recommend books and audio programs by authors such as Gary Renard and Ken Wapnick, as these will undoubtedly facilitate your understanding of the Course's material (see resources section). If you are already familiar with *A Course in Miracles* and are confident that you have a sound understanding of its principles, feel free to skip this section.

Part 2 offers a primer on hypnosis, hypnotherapy and hypno-psychotherapy. You will discover the power of the subconscious mind, and how hypnotherapists leverage it to help their clients resolve issues. I will

vi

describe hypnosis, debunk its myths and cover the most common professional hypnotherapy techniques. This is merely an overview of this vast subject, and aims to cover only the topics that are relevant to further chapters of the book.

In this section, I will also teach you self-hypnosis, how to design your own sessions, and how to apply the techniques you will learn in part 3.

Part 3 will apply hypnotherapy techniques to the spiritual practice. I will discuss the parallels between the teachings of *A Course in Miracles* and the techniques used in hypnotherapy, and examine how states of hypnosis seem to take us closer to our true Selves. You will see how hypnosis may give you a glimpse of what true Oneness may be like.

You will also learn ways to use hypnotherapy to facilitate your application of the Course's principles, and accelerate your spiritual growth. *A Course in Miracles'* approach is very different from most other spiritual paths, and although easy to understand on an intellectual level, the principles are sometimes difficult to readily assimilate and practice in our daily lives. This is exactly where hypnotherapy techniques excel: removing bad habits or building good ones at the subconscious level. Hypno-analysis can also help release unresolved, unconscious emotional issues, which are often preventing people from taking the next step in their spiritual journey.

Each chapter will cover a different aspect of the Course's teachings, and for each topic, you will learn how to use hypnosis to better apply the corresponding principle.

vii

Introduction

Practical step-by-step hypnotherapy exercises are provided throughout and marked with the following symbol:

Note that all these exercises involve getting into a state of hypnosis. So, do not attempt them while driving or doing any other activity that requires attention. Only perform them when you can relax and focus on the exercise.

I have also included client case studies to illustrate the application of techniques to specific issues. The names of the clients have been changed to protect the privacy of the individuals.

IMPORTANT NOTE

I contend that, by using hypnotherapeutic techniques, you can more easily accept and practice the principles of *A Course in Miracles*. However, these should not be considered as a substitute for reading the Course and practicing the workbook exercises. This book is merely an aid and should only be considered as a means to an end to help you achieve faster results.

PART 1
-
INTRODUCTION TO
A COURSE IN MIRACLES

CHAPTER ONE

-

OVERVIEW OF A COURSE IN MIRACLES

In this section, I will provide an overview of the key concepts of *A Course in Miracles,* which will arm you with the basic knowledge necessary to understand the practical advice and exercises given in part 3.

Once again, this should not be considered as a substitute for reading the Course and practicing the exercises in the Workbook.

Note: The Course presents fairly unconventional ideas that may make some people uncomfortable since they go against what they have been brought up to believe. There have therefore been different interpretations and misunderstandings of the Course. Some Course teachers choose (purposely or because of their own unconscious fears) to present a watered-down version of the Course, which may be easier to accept for the average person, but misses some of the critical aspects that are essential for the correct application of its principles. I follow a stricter, uncompromising interpretation of the Course, based on the teachings of Ken Wapnick, the main original editor of the Course.

Overview of A Course in Miracles

HOW THE COURSE CAME ABOUT

A Course in Miracles is a spiritual text published in 1976, which describes a radically different approach to spirituality. Although it names no official author, it was the result of the work of Helen Schucman and Bill Thetford, two psychotherapists working at *Columbia Presbyterian Medical Center*.

Though their personalities were opposed, they joined together to work towards a common goal (what the Course would describe as a "holy instant"). Frustrated by the animosity they encountered in their working relationship, they sought to find a "better way". Helen started receiving a series of visions and dreams. She also began hearing a voice – which identified itself as Jesus – asking her to take notes. After much initial resistance, Helen began to take shorthand notes of the monologue. She would then read these notes to Bill, who would type them. This took place over a period of around 7 years.

Helen scribed 3 books:
- A text, which contains the theory and principles of the Course
- A workbook for students, which contains 365 lessons with exercises to practice the principles
- A manual for teachers, which forms a good summary of the principles

There are also 3 addendums:
- Clarification of Terms
- Psychotherapy Pamphlet
- Song of Prayers

INTENT

A Course in Miracles is not a religion or a cult; its teachings describe a practical path to enable individuals to find their way back to God. It does not claim to be the only way. There are thousands of valid spiritual paths that all lead to the same outcome, but *A Course in Miracles* does claim to speed up the process.

A Course in Miracles is not for everybody. It will resonate with some people, and those for which it does not resonate will find another spiritual path that suits them better.

Jesus' message from 2,000 years ago has been greatly misunderstood and distorted. The Bible and Christianity came long after his passing. They have been used to divide instead of unite, and have generated hatred and atrocities (e.g. Spanish Inquisition) and wars (e.g. the Crusades), thereby accomplishing the opposite of Jesus' original teachings. This time, He does not want His message to be distorted; that's why *A Course in Miracles* was "written" by Him rather than someone else.

The core message is love, which comes through forgiveness and seeing shared interest.

TERMINOLOGY

The Course uses Christian terminology, mainly because it is addressed to a western, mostly Christian (though not very Christ-like in its behavior) audience. It aims to correct errors in Christianity and the misunderstanding of Jesus' original message. It contains many references to the Bible and reinterpretations of its

Overview of A Course in Miracles

meaning. Though the words are Christian, the meaning that the Course gives to them is very different. Words such as *miracle, atonement, sin, Jesus, God, Holy Spirit,* etc. have different connotations, as I will describe below.

Also, the concepts described really cannot be put into meaningful words as "words are but symbols of symbols, therefore twice removed from reality" (M-21.10). So, the Course uses terms of our own world to communicate to us what is essentially impossible to describe. That's why the literal meaning of any particular passage is irrelevant. What is important is the content of the message, not its style or form. The form in *A Course in Miracles* is actually inconsistent, because it uses symbols, concepts and words, which are inherently illusory and inaccurate. The Course does not have to be believed or analyzed, but experienced.

If the Christian terms used in the Course (or the fact that *Jesus* is the alleged inspiration for the book) bother you, feel free to substitute your own words. You can call this symbolic spiritual guide Jesus, Holy Spirit, Buddha, Joanna, Bubba, Billy Bob or whatever you want. For simplicity, this book will keep with the Course terms. Once again, what matters is the content, not the form. But, also realize that it would be a good exercise to examine why these terms upset you, and a good forgiveness opportunity.

◆

The Course also borrows terms from psychology. For instance, it often refers to the *ego*. The word "ego", as used by Freud, is one part of the psyche (along with the *id* and *superego*). In the Course, it's closer to the whole psyche and represents the self. As we will see, the ego represents the wrong-minded thought system that keeps us rooted in the world. *A Course in Miracles* shows us that Freud's mistake was to not realize that the ego is a defense against God and our true Self. But, Freud was spot-on with his analysis of how the ego defends against fear and guilt.

◆

Some people have taken offense to the fact that the Course uses masculine pronouns (as opposed to the fashionable and politically correct "he or she") and masculine terms (such as Father, Son, etc.). As we'll discuss in the chapter "Face lift", people are always on the lookout for any sign of victimization and a reason to feel offended. This masculine/feminine debate is a perfect example of it. The Course's message is clearly one of oneness and inclusion, so it is absurd to claim it is sexist because of this particular grammar use. If this style offends you, feel free to mentally replace "he" by "he or she", but also consider this an opportunity to examine the source of this upset and forgive yourself for it.

Following the Course's convention, this book will also use masculine pronouns and terms.

◆

There is also a debate regarding whether the person consulting a therapist should be called "patient" or "client". In the traditional medical profession, "patient" is commonly used, but in the complementary therapy arena (of which hypnotherapy is part), "client" is usually the accepted term and I will use it in this book as well.

Overview of A Course in Miracles

CENTRAL MESSAGE

The Course follows a pure non-dualistic philosophy, which means that there is God and nothing else (anything else is an illusion). This contrasts sharply with the more traditional dualistic doctrines (such as Christianity), where God is on one side of the "fence" and we mere mortals are on the other (with the hope to move to the other side one day).

So, according to the Course, the world we experience is an illusion. In reality, we are (and always have been) One with God, and are living a dream of sorts. Indeed, if God is perfect, limitless, changeless, formless and eternal, what He creates must also be. But, since nothing in the universe has these characteristics, the only logical conclusion is that it was not created by God and therefore is not real. The Course teaches us that, through forgiveness and recognizing shared interest, we can start to undo our mistaken perception, and eventually go back to the Oneness which we think we left.

This mistaken perception of what reality is reminds me of Plato's allegory of the cave. In this metaphor, prisoners are chained in a cave and restrained from moving or turning their head. They face a blank wall on the cave. In the back of the cave, behind the prisoners is a large fire and a walkway on which people pass by, carrying shapes and figures. The prisoners only see the shadows cast on the wall and hear echoes off the wall. Since they have been chained there since childhood, this is all they know and they think the shadows are reality. They play games trying to predict which shape will appear next, and the most talented of them at that game are considered clever and wise.

Now, imagine one of the prisoners breaks free of his shackles, stands up and looks back. At first, he would be frightened of or even deny what he sees and be blinded by the fire's light. His temptation would be to go back to the comforting safety of what he's used to. Over time, his eyes might adjust to the light and he can start realizing that the shadows are not reality but just a reflection of it. He can venture out of the cave and once his eyes have adjusted to the sun's brightness, can discover what the world is really like.

If he then goes back to the cave to tell his former companions about what he discovered, how the shadows on the wall are unreal, and how the games they play are irrelevant, they will consider him crazy and ridicule him since what he is recounting is so contrary to what they are accustomed to.

The following sections describe how the illusion came about, how we behave in the illusion, and how we can get out of the illusion according to the Course.

HOW DID WE (APPEAR TO) GET HERE?

This section describes the "mythology" of the Course. Though symbolic, metaphorical and illusory, this mythology helps to explain the principles behind the Course.

What we call reality is, in fact, an illusion. Our *true* reality (what we are and have always been) is what is called One-Mindedness. It is the Oneness of God (which is pure spirit, changeless, formless and eternal) and Christ (God's one Son). Though we do not perceive it that way, we are actually Christ, as we will see in a

Overview of A Course in Miracles

moment (but we are not God; we are not the *Source* of being). The Mind of God and Christ (the Son) are one, with no clear delineation of where one ends and the other begins.

In that perfect Oneness, came a "tiny mad idea" where the Son of God thought he could be separate from God. Though just an idea, the Son of God took it seriously and believed the thought was capable of real effects. So, it seemed as though He was able to separate from perfect Oneness (which in reality could never happen). The moment when the Son of God thought he could separate from God, He set up the new thought system of the ego, who looked at the tiny mad idea and relished in the newfound freedom and individuality. Immediately, God "sent" the correction in the form of the Holy Spirit. The Holy Spirit is the Right Mind, the memory of who we are and can be thought of as the link between God and his (seemingly) separated Son. The principle of the Atonement is the realization that the separation never happened and is the central tenet of the Course.

Note that when I say "God sent the correction", it is really a metaphor. God knows nothing of this; if He did, it would mean that He acknowledges the separation really happened, which would contradict the endless nature of Oneness. Also, keep in mind that "Holy Spirit" and "ego" are just thoughts in our mind and not actual entities.

We, therefore, have two mutually exclusive ways of looking at the "tiny mad idea" (the ego's and the Holy Spirit's) and a "decision maker" who needs to choose between the two systems: between being individual (ego) and being part of the whole (Holy Spirit).

At this point, the mind is severely split, and the decision maker's view is skewed towards the ego. We no

10

longer pay attention to the Holy Spirit and the decision maker's choice to back the ego becomes deeply hidden. In order to ensure its "survival", the ego makes a plan to make sure the decision maker never changes his mind, by making him forget he even *has* a mind.

To that effect, the ego makes up a "horror story", and tells the Son that he is a terrible person, has sinned against his Father, and that if he stays in his mind, he will be destroyed by God. The Son of God is overwhelmed with guilt for what He (thinks He) has done and becomes fearful that God will punish him for his sin (the sin of destroying Oneness and essentially taking God's life). So, the ego leads the Son of God into a world where they can "hide", and where He will not be punished or destroyed. "God will never find us here", says the ego. Thus is the world created and we (the Sonship) start separating into billions and billions of fragments. To ensure we never get back to the decision maker, we convince ourselves that the world and the body are real, and that God interacts with it. So, we stay mindless (the Bible is all about the body and the state of mindlessness) in order to not have to face the guilt that is deeply buried within us.

The Mind has now been pushed out and replaced by the split mind: which consists of both the right mind and wrong mind.

We are now so identified with the ego and the world that we forget all about the decision we made and the fact that this is all an illusion. It's a little like Orson Wells' "The War of the Worlds", a radio drama broadcast in 1938, based on HG Wells novel of the same name. At the beginning of the program, Wells warned the audience that what they were about to hear was a fictitious story. The program then consisted of a series

Overview of A Course in Miracles

news flashes describing the invasion of Earth by Martians. The show was very well done and realistic and, to the people who missed the disclaimer at the beginning, it seemed real and frightening, and caused a certain level of panic among the population. Well, our life is similar to that story. We missed (or forgot) the disclaimer at the beginning that this is all made up and believe what we see and what is happening to us in the world is real, so we take the fictitious story seriously. Jesus (or the Holy Spirit) is the gentle constant reminder of that disclaimer. But few hear it or believe it.

So, in summary, we now have 3 thought systems:
- one-mindedness: the pure spirit God/Christ that is our reality
- wrong-mindedness: the thought system of the ego , the body and the world we see
- right-mindedness: the thought system of the Holy Spirit, which is our "link" to God

Only the first one is real, the other two are illusory.

LEVELS

The Course is written on 2 levels:
- Level 1 is the metaphysical level. Here, the world and body are regarded as illusions and represent the separation from God.
- Level 2 relates to this world, in which we appear to be. World and body are neutral and can serve the purpose of ego (reinforce separation) or Holy

Spirit (as a teaching device through which to learn forgiveness lessons).

It's important to realize that the Course itself is part of the ego framework. The Course talks to us as if we were actually here. The "you" it addresses is the decision maker, and not the individual self that we think we are. It meets us where we think we are and leads us to where we truly are.

Another important distinction to make is form versus content. Whatever happens on the level of form in this world does not matter. All correction and healing happens in the mind. It is crucial to not mix the two, otherwise you risk misinterpreting the Course completely. For instance, the content of an interaction could be love, but the form it takes in the world may not necessarily appear loving (and vice-versa).

METAPHORICAL LANGUAGE

It's important to note that *A Course in Miracles* makes heavy use of metaphorical language. The reader needs to keep that in mind to avoid interpreting references literally. The Course uses analogies and metaphors to express ideas that cannot really be put into words. It addresses us at the level we (think we) are. The crucial point to remember is that the Course is a non-dualistic system (there's God and Christ in Oneness and everything else is unreal). So, any reference in the Course that seems to indicate that God actively acts in the world, interacts with us, misses us, etc. should be interpreted metaphorically. If God really did

13

acknowledge the world and the separation, it would make the error real and, in effect, affirm duality.

CHAPTER TWO

-

RIGHT OR WRONG

As we have seen, there are two diametrically opposed thought systems: the ego's and the Holy Spirit's. In this chapter, I will describe these two systems, their origin and their effects on us.

WRONG-MINDEDNESS:
THE EGO THOUGHT SYSTEM

As we discussed in the previous chapter, the ego thought system began when we believed we established a self autonomous from God (original sin). Once we thought we had sinned, we experienced a tremendous guilt. The "guilt" we experience in our everyday lives is not attached to something specific, but is a reflection of this original guilt. It refers to the sum of all our negative feelings, beliefs and experiences. Guilt can be in the form of self-hatred or self-rejection (such as feelings of incompetence, failure, emptiness) or feelings that some things are lacking in us. Most of it is unconscious. However it manifests, the ultimate source of guilt is our belief we separated from God.

Right or Wrong

The guilt we experienced over the separation generated fear that God would punish us for our *sin*. All worldly fears really come from being afraid of this punishment. The biblical God is portrayed as vengeful and wrathful. The real God is actually a God of love and would, of course, never exert the type of vicious vengeance described in the Bible.

Nobody could live with this level of self-hatred, guilt and fear. And, since we think God is now our enemy, we turn to the ego for help. Unfortunately, the ego has its own agenda, and his help is really only geared towards keeping himself alive and well. The ego only cares about keeping us rooted in the world, so that we do not realize we have the power to make another choice. It does not care whether we experience pain or pleasure, as long as we experience something outside of ourselves. Its biggest fear is not of God or the Holy Spirit, but of our realization that we can choose again (and choose against it this time).

PROJECTION AND THE CYCLE OF GUILT

A key concept in the Course is the notion of projection, that is the idea that we're taking something inside ourselves and projecting it onto someone else, so that it's "not my fault" but someone else's. We internally say "you're the guilty person, not me". Once we've repressed our guilt and projected it onto others, we attack it by our anger or judgment of them. But, we are really seeing something in them that is in us (since there is nothing outside of us). This is a metaphor similar to the one described in Leviticus, where the high priest would "attach" all the sins of the village to a goat and symbolically cast it out of the village (the origins of the expression *scapegoat*).

So, it *seems* that we can get rid of our guilt by projecting it. The problem is that this projection is really the best way to actually feel *more* guilty, because we cannot attack someone (physically or in thought) without feeling guilty about it. And that's exactly what the ego wants. The ego is just a belief in separation. If we were to realize that we're not guilty (because the separation did not occur), the ego would disappear. So, it tries to keep us feeling guilty. To that effect, the ego sets up a vicious circle: the more guilt we feel, the more we attack, and therefore the more guilt we feel. A brilliant plan!

Once we have attacked another person, we feel guilty, think we deserve punishment for the attack, and fear that the other will attack us back. Whether they do or not, we defend against it. And, since we've repressed our guilt, any attack against us seems unjustified. The more we defend ourselves, the more we (subconsciously) convince ourselves that we're guilty, and here is a vicious circle again. This is the reason for any conflict in the world: from the nuclear arms race to more mundane escalations in our daily lives.

In our effort to find scapegoats to projects our guilt onto, we divide up the world into good and bad groups. We strive to find people who are different and not as "good" as us. Even religions have been dividing and subdividing for ages. We have an investment in seeing the "bad guy" lose, as it releases us of our sins... or so we think.

Right or Wrong

SPECIAL RELATIONSHIPS

An important aspect of the wrong-minded thought system is the notion of special relationships. They can take two forms: special hate and special love.

- *Special hate* relationships occur when we find someone to blame, so we can escape the true object of our hate: ourselves. This is the cycle of guilt described previously.

- *Special love* relationships are more insidious and subtle. The concept of scarcity is at play here; it relies on our feeling that something is lacking in us. The ego suggests we look outside ourselves for that something or someone who can fill that lack and meet our special need. When we find that person, we love them; and if we fill their lack and meet their special need too, they love us back. This is, of course, not the love of the Holy Spirit, but more akin to a co-dependency.

This special love does not only apply to people; it can also apply to substances (alcohol, drugs, food, etc.) or things (clothes, cars, money, status, etc.). The trick is that special relationships are only there to meet a *perceived* need, and therefore the other person/substance/thing becomes a symbol and a reminder of our own guilt. If the person starts to change and no longer meet our need (or not fill our lack as much), we begin to feel our guilt resurfacing. We try to change them back by making them feel guilty about their change. If the other person does not change back, our love begins to turn to anger and hate, because we cannot stand to deal with our own guilt. We then search for the next relationship in which to hide this guilt.

But, only by letting go of the guilt would a relationship really be based on love (in the true meaning of the word). Also, by using others to meet our needs, we deny their identity as Christ, and therefore reinforce the ego in us. This form of attack makes us feel guilty, which reinforces the cycle.

A relationship is "holy" and not "special" when it is not at the expense of anyone else. In other words, the degree to which we exclude others is how we can measure the specialness of our relationships.

RIGHT-MINDEDNESS - THE HOLY SPIRIT'S THOUGHT SYSTEM

The prime concept of right-mindedness is that we are already healed and guiltless, and we just need to accept that fact. To help us achieve this realization, the Holy Spirit turns the table on the ego by using the same projections to teach us forgiveness and allow us to release our guilt. Since we've projected our sin and guilt onto others, by forgiving them, we are really forgiving ourselves. This is the central tenet of the Course.

Therefore, by seeing the light of Christ in others, we see it in ourselves. The people who cause us the most trouble are, in fact, our best opportunities to realize that the guilt is in us, and for us to make a new choice – a choice to see the person or situation through the Holy Spirit's eyes, thereby ridding ourselves of the associated guilt.

So, the first step to forgiveness is realizing the problem is not outside of us but inside – in our mind.

Right or Wrong

The ego will do all it can to keep us from accepting this idea, by finding other people (parents, spouse, co-workers, politicians, world leaders, sports teams, etc.) or things (the weather, an illness, pollution, etc.) to blame outside of us, rather than in our mind. Actually, it endeavors to keep us from realizing we even *have* a mind: if we don't know we have a mind, how can we change it?

Once we have accepted the attack is a decision that we made to project our guilt, the next step is to look at that guilt we made up and realize that it's not who we are. As the Son of God, we are guiltless. This step of facing our guilt seems easy in theory, but in reality is extremely difficult and takes time to reach. We cannot remove the guilt by ourselves; we can only make the *decision* to get rid of it, and need to "ask" the Holy Spirit to take it away, which He does in a way that is appropriate. In reality, He already has (as there was no guilt in the first place), but we have not accepted this fact yet.

This process is deceptively easy; it takes a long time to get rid of all the guilt. We need to do it one part at a time, and usually many lifetimes are necessary. Once a "lesson" is learned, that part of the guilt is removed and we can move to another one. Note that when I say "a part of guilt is removed", this is really a metaphor to help in understanding the process. In reality, we're not literally chipping away at guilt or at the ego. The ego thought system remains unchanged and the Holy Spirit thought system remains the same as well. We just keep switching between the two thought systems and, over time, we align more and more often with the Holy Spirit side.

The Course is challenging as it goes against everything we've been brought up to believe. It describes what's wrong with the ego, and since we're strongly identified with it, we fight the Course's teachings.

An alternative way to look at the central message of the Course is to understand that salvation comes from joining, which means seeing shared interests with others. When two people "join" to share a common interest or work for a common goal, this constitutes a "holy instant". This always involves forgiveness. The joining of Helen and Bill during the transcription of the Course is the perfect illustration of this concept. Note that the joining I am talking about is at the level of mind. Simply getting together as a group in the physical world does not necessarily constitute joining.

◆

In this chapter, I discussed the concepts of right-mindedness and wrong-mindedness, as well as the notion of special relationships.

In the next chapter, I will summarize the key concepts of the Course and describe how to apply them to our everyday life.

CHAPTER THREE

-

KEY CONCEPTS

In this chapter, we move away from the theory and mythology, and examine how the Course principles apply to our lives. In part 3, we will delve deeper into these aspects, and see how hypnotherapy can aid us in applying these principles more consistently by installing them deeper in our mind at a subconscious level.

A CALL FOR LOVE

In our everyday lives, we are confronted with attacks, some physical, some verbal, some psychological, many imaginary. We usually react by fighting back (by making others feel guilty about how much they make us suffer, or by attacking them back). But, if we're in our right mind, we know we're the Son of God, God loves us and nothing can hurt us. At the same time, we can be aware that the "attacker" clearly does not know that he too is the Son of God, and is loved by God. So, his attack is, in fact, a *call* for love (the love he thinks he does not have or is not deserving of). When in our right mind, what we're hearing is "teach me that I'm wrong and that I'm really loved". So, the only response we can have is one of love. The exact form of this love does not matter and will

Key Concepts

be driven by the Holy Spirit, if we ask Him (see Chapter 15 for details). Note that the love may not necessarily be manifested by any "action" in the world, as it only has to do with our mind.

So everything we encounter in the world is either an expression of love or a call for love; to which, either way, the response is always love. Once again, we do not need to know what to do specifically, but we just need to ask the Holy Spirit for help in guiding us to the most loving thing to do.

Therefore, we can see every event or person in our life (especially the more difficult ones) as an opportunity to forgive and express love, thereby healing our own guilt. As discussed previously, because our guilt is projected outside of ourselves and into the world around us, it is by the forgiveness of all things that we ourselves are forgiven. Therefore, excluding someone from this love means leaving part of our guilt unhealed.

MIRACLES

The word "miracle", as used in the Course, has nothing to do with the usual meaning of the word, such as walking on water, curing people of diseases or anything external. Miracles are an internal phenomenon. They represent a correction, the undoing of a false perception. So, healing occurs when there's a shift in perception (through *true* forgiveness). The miracle occurs, for instance, when you change your hatred of someone to love, which means you look at the person or situation through the Holy Spirit's eyes, instead of the ego's, and become aware of the call for love.

24

It is crucial to understand that the goal of "living" *A Course in Miracles* is to live our lives in alignment with love. It is not to change the world or others, but just to change our own *mind* about them and let the Holy Spirit do whatever He thinks is best. So, we never really forgive directly: we *choose* to allow the Holy Spirit's forgiveness to come through us, and through this forgiveness is our guilt released.

The path we follow is individualized. The Holy Spirit plans how we will correct our specific errors and "sends" people to help us, the ultimate goal being the realization that the one who can really help us is inside us (in our mind). Once again, since events and the world are all illusory, the Holy Spirit does not actually "send" anyone; this is a metaphor used in the Course to express teachings in terms familiar to us.

Looking at the world through the Holy Spirit's eyes is the key. When separation occurred (or seemed to occur), the metaphorical carpet of time rolled out, and we started walking along it, further and further from God. The ego takes us down the carpet, away from God, while the Holy Spirit rolls the carpet back.

Another useful analogy is driving a car. The driver (the decision maker, i.e. you) can either put the car shifter in "Drive" and move forward (the way of the Holy Spirit, which takes you towards Oneness) or in "Reverse" (the way of the ego which takes you away from your real Self). These are the only two choices and we cannot be simultaneously in Drive and Reverse mode. Of course, we change gear a lot in our daily lives, and constantly alternate between going forward and backward. But, over time, we go forward more and more often, until we reach our destination (or rather, we

Key Concepts

realize we were asleep and dreaming at the wheel, and actually never left our starting point).

As we get closer to the core of the ego, we get very afraid of having to face our guilt, and the ego "attacks" us because it sees our alignment with the Holy Spirit as a betrayal. That's why we need to take it slow and remember we have someone loving us and holding our hand through the process, a friendly driving instructor sitting by our side, reminding us gently of the gear to choose. It does not matter whether you call this symbolic supporting presence Jesus, Buddha, Holy Spirit or anything else (all are illusory after all). What is important is to know that He's there with you, whether or not you are aware of it consciously.

LIVING IN PEACE

Another key challenge for us is to change our image of ourselves to that of the Son that God created, invulnerable and who cannot be hurt by anything or anyone.

Initially, the goal of the process is not to awaken from the dream entirely, but to live our life in a state of constant peace regardless of what happens, with no guilt to project. We don't have to agree with everybody, but we should not let that disagreement be the base for attacks and forgetting all Sons of God are one.

We should also take care not to substitute rituals of love for the *experience* of love, as Christianity and most formal religions have done. The universal experience in heaven is love; forgiveness is its reflection in this world.

We do not have to accept the Course's theory, theology or cosmology, but we need to use them to experience the unity of the Sonship. The experience of forgiveness is what we truly want, and it's important to not let theology get in the way, and certainly not use it as a weapon against those who do not believe in it.

Let's remember that we do not save the world by our deeds, but by healing our own inner mind. Since all minds are joined, when we're healed, the mind of the Sonship is healed. And, since the world comes from the mind, it is healed too (and eventually disappears).

SUMMARY OF KEY PRINCIPLES

In summary, the key points to remember are:
- This world is an illusion, a dream of separation from God that could never happen
- You have a split mind: ego (wrong-minded thoughts) and Holy Spirit (right-minded thoughts)
- You have the power to decide between the two parts of your mind
- You can choose to see the world through the eyes of the ego by:
  - portraying yourself as an innocent victim
  - seeing everyone as separate from you
  - buying into special relationships
  - living in fear of being punished for your "sins"
- You can decide for the Holy Spirit's view by
  - Seeing shared interest and joining (at the level of mind) with others
  - Staying at peace in your mind regardless of what external events seem to occur

Key Concepts

- o Forgiving others (and therefore yourself) for what they have *not* done
- o Accepting the Atonement for yourself (i.e. the separation never happened)
- o Recognizing your identity as Christ instead of your current earthly identity
- o Seeing the world as a school, where you can learn forgiveness lessons and undo your guilt
- o Making each relationship a "holy" one
- The goal of the Course is not to be ego-less, anger-less and upset-less, but to acknowledge your ego, anger and upset, and look at them without judgment.

◆

Figure 1 summarizes the Course's principles and its metaphysics. It depicts the various "minds" and the keywords associated with each.

Hypnotic Spirituality

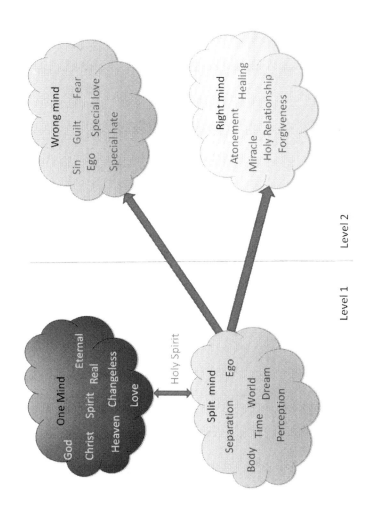

Figure 1

Key Concepts

QUOTATION REFERENCES

Throughout this book, whenever a passage from the Course is quoted, I will indicate the reference to that passage using the following standard notation.

First is a letter:
- T for Text
- W for Workbook
- M for Manual for Teachers

For the Text, the notation will be:
T-Chapter.Section.Paragraph:Sentence
For example: T-26.IV.4:7

For the Workbook, the notation will be:
W-Part.Lesson.Paragraph:Sentence
For example: W-pI.169.5:2

For the Manual for Teacher, the notation will be:
M-Question number.Paragraph:Sentence
For example: M-13.3:2

PART 2
-
OVERVIEW OF HYPNOSIS AND HYPNOTHERAPY

INTRODUCTION

There is much misunderstanding regarding hypnosis. It is not a new concept; in fact, it has been around for many thousands of years, and contrary to the belief of many, it is a totally natural phenomenon and is perfectly safe and usually profoundly beneficial. But, only recently has its use become more common in the complementary therapy arena.

Hypnotherapy uses hypnosis as a therapeutic aid. It has been used to assist people in overcoming many issues, ranging from emotional trauma to stopping smoking, losing weight, improving sports performance, relieving fears and phobias, etc. There's even the possibility of healing on a cellular level, which could be of benefit to sufferers of many physical diseases, including cancer.

The most compelling argument for hypnotherapy is the relative speed of treatment. What could take ten years of weekly psychotherapy sessions can often be achieved in relatively few hypnotherapy sessions. This is because hypnotherapy utilizes the power of the subconscious mind, instead of dealing purely at the level of the conscious mind (see chapter 5 for details on the conscious and subconscious minds).

Introduction

In this section, I will introduce you to hypnosis and hypnotherapy. We will discuss the history, myths and techniques of hypnotherapy. This section is not intended to provide a full coverage of this vast subject, but will arm you with enough knowledge to understand part 3, where we will apply the techniques to the spiritual practice.

You will also learn self-hypnosis techniques so you can do your own hypnosis sessions.

CHAPTER FOUR
-
BRIEF HISTORY

Hypnotic or suggestive therapy has been used as a healing technique for a very long time. References to it can be found in the Bible, and it was of prime importance in the "sleep temples" of Ancient Greece - which were places of pilgrimage and healing. In the Middle-Ages, beliefs in miraculous cures associated with religious shrines were widespread and healing was brought about by touch and prayer.

◆

The modern use of hypnotherapy began during the 18th century, when the theory of "Magnetism" was developed by Franz Anton Mesmer (1734-1815). He argued that the planets influenced mankind through their magnetic effects on the "fluid" which occupied all of space. He presented a theory that these magnetic "fluids" were responsible for disease and could also heal the body. So, he started using magnets to heal people. He relied on passing magnets around a distressed person, and later simply making passes with his hands.

His methods were extremely successful, and his popularity soared, to the point where he was unable to keep up with the demand for his services. He then

Brief history

started to "magnetize" objects, which his patients could touch to find the relief they sought from their symptoms.

Mesmer became famous after the publication of his account of *Animal Magnetism* in 1775, and he started work at the famous "Paris Salon" during the 1780s. Unfortunately, he started to embellish his abilities, and when investigated by the French Government in 1784, his ideas were soon discredited and he was labeled a fraud. The French Royal Commission dismissed the cures they observed by explaining them away as caused by the imaginations of the subjects. The positive results of Mesmer's work were overlooked by the Commission, along with the fact that many people were indeed cured by his methods. Of course, the Commission was right in the sense that what cured people was not Mesmer or his magnets, but their *belief* that they would be cured.

◆

In the late 18th century, the Marquis de Puységur, one of Mesmer's students, used "magnetic somnambulism" (magnetic sleepwalking) as a clinical technique. This linked mesmerism with the psychic world. Puységur is known for his discovery of three main features of hypnosis:

- concentration of the senses on the operator
- acceptance of suggestion without question
- amnesia of events in a trance.

◆

In the first half of the 19th century, John Elliotson (1791-1868), a professor of theory and practice at the University Hospital in London, and president of the

Hypnotic Spirituality

Royal Medical and Surgical Society of London, reported using hypnosis as anesthesia in major surgical operations (this was before chemical anesthesia was available).

James Braid (1795-1860), a prominent Scottish surgeon, re-examined Mesmerism. He named the phenomenon "Hypnosis" (after the Greek god of sleep, *Hypnos*). Later in his life, he realized that hypnosis was not really sleep, but concentration of the mind. However, by then, the term "hypnosis" had become the known and accepted name. So, his attempt to change it to "Monoidiesm" failed.

Meanwhile, James Esdaile (1808-1859), a Scottish surgeon in India, reported performing several thousand surgeries – at least 300 of them major, including amputations – using only hypnosis as anesthesia.

Esdaile discovered the so-called "coma" state, a depth of trance below that of somnambulism, where people experience feelings of total bliss and euphoria (see chapter 5 for details). However, when Esdaile returned to the U.K., he found that the general lack of belief and expectation meant that his methods failed.

◆

In the late 19th century, Sigmund Freud (1856-1939) – known mainly for his psycho-analytical techniques and the discovery of free association – used hypnosis for a while in his therapy. He wasn't a particularly good hypnotist, but he helped bring hypnosis into the mainstream of discussion. Later in his life, he abandoned the use of hypnosis, but continued to use some of hypnotherapy's basic techniques in his work.

Brief history

As psychoanalysis grew in popularity, hypnosis fell out of favor for decades, and its use as an anesthetic was quickly superseded by chemical methods.

◆

In the early part of the 20th century, hypnosis was used almost exclusively by stage hypnotists. Although these hypnotists managed to keep the art alive, the entertainment factor did distort the general public's view of this very powerful therapeutic tool. However, many of these entertainers understood the power of their art and began using hypnosis off-stage to help people overcome issues such as shyness or stuttering, and to change bad habits.

Dave Elman (1900-1967) helped bring hypnotherapy to the attention of the medical community in the mid-20th century, by teaching hypnosis to many medical professionals. He is well known for having invented a fast induction method which enabled, in just a few minutes, states of hypnosis deep enough for surgery.

In the 1950s, The British Medical Association and the American Medical Association issued statements supporting the usefulness of hypnosis as a form of therapy. The British Medical Association endorsed the practice of hypnosis in Medical School education. Since then, it had become a valuable addition to conventional medical treatment. In 1962, a brain operation was even performed under hypnosis in Indianapolis.

Milton Erickson (1901-1980), a renowned psycho-therapist, was perhaps the most important influence on the acceptance of hypnotherapy in the 20th century. Erickson was a master of hypnosis, and worked intuitively. He designed a great deal of the hypnotic

Hypnotic Spirituality

language patterns still used today. The main areas he felt a therapist needed to concentrate on were language, ambiguity, metaphors and rapport.

In 1991, The British Medical Association reported favorably on the use of hypnosis in the field of medicine. Furthermore, a study in the New Scientist Magazine (vol 136 issue 1845) also concluded that hypnosis is the most effective method to quit smoking.

However, despite the evidence of the efficacy of hypnosis, medical training incorporates very little of this vast field of study. Therefore, hypnosis is not practiced widely by medical professionals. And there is still a stigma and a prejudice towards hypnosis in the medical profession, and a preference for the use of drugs (due in large part to the influence of pharmaceutical lobbies).

So, today the art of hypnotherapy is offered mostly by "lay practitioners.

CHAPTER FIVE

-

INTRODUCTION TO HYPNOTHERAPY

In this section, I'll discuss the basics of hypnosis, the subconscious mind, the various levels of trance and the role of the therapist.

AN OCCULT ART OR A NATURAL PHENOMENON?

Hypnosis is one of the most misunderstood phenomena. Some people associate it with occult practices, and consider hypnotists to be voodoo magicians with mystical powers capable of making people obey their commands and do their bidding. This is probably due, in part, to the influence of stage hypnotists who, for dramatic effect, portray hypnosis as a supernatural and mystical event.

In reality, hypnosis is a very natural state that we all experience every day. For instance, have you ever driven somewhere and, upon arrival, realized that there were periods when your mind was somewhere else and you did not remember the details of parts of your journey? Or have you ever been so absorbed in a book, a movie or a conversation with a friend that the world around you

Introduction to hypnotherapy

just seemed to disappear? Or have you ever caught yourself simply day-dreaming? In all these situations, you were in a state of hypnosis.

DEFINITION

There isn't an officially agreed-upon definition of hypnosis. But, most people agree that hypnosis is an altered state of consciousness, a focused state of attention where suggestibility is increased.

Contrary to popular belief, and despite what the name seems to imply (given that the *hypnos* root means sleep), hypnosis is not a sleep state. It is a conscious waking state in which one is able to bring oneself back to a normal waking state at any time during the trance experience. Subjects remain conscious and alert, though the focused state of attention on one idea or one concept, usually results in them being less aware of their surroundings.

During a hypnosis session with a professional hypnotherapist, clients remain conscious and able to communicate verbally. The ability to talk is actually a crucial part of some forms of hypnotherapy as we will see.

WHAT DOES IT FEEL LIKE?

There is no "standard" feeling of hypnosis. Different people experience it in different ways. Most people will feel very relaxed. Some feel a tingling sensation. Some feel a bit cold or warm. Some feel a little numbness. Some feel their body getting heavy, others feel very light (as though they are floating sometimes). And some feel nothing particular at all.

As there is really no such thing as a "hypnotized feeling", every person's experience is equally valid. I always remind my clients that they really can't get it wrong. All that is necessary for someone to experience hypnosis is for them to want to do so and allow themselves to drift into this peaceful state, either by themselves or guided by someone else.

WHAT IS IT GOOD FOR?

Hypnotherapy uses hypnosis for therapeutic purposes. For example, to achieve positive changes such as overcoming negative habits or improving some aspect of themselves, such as confidence. The therapist leverages the resources available in their clients to help them accomplish their goals.

Hypnotherapy has been used to help people with a variety of psychological, emotional or psycho-somatic issues. It can also help with medical issues, under referral from a licensed physician.

The most common applications of hypnotherapy are:

- Removing a bad habit (smoking, nail biting, etc.)
- Removing a fear or phobia (fear of flying, elevators, spiders, etc.)
- Enhancing an ability such as improving a golf swing or the accuracy of a free throw
- Improving confidence and self-esteem
- Obsessive thoughts
- Relieving ill-feelings such as anxiety, jealousy, anger, guilt, etc.

Introduction to hypnotherapy

- Investigating fertility issues and aiding natural birthing
- Weight issues

THE POWER OF THE SUBCONSCIOUS

The human mind is made up of two main parts: the conscious and the subconscious. The subconscious mind is much more powerful and its power is largely untapped by most people. It stores information as we learn, and controls our behaviors as these are all based on past feelings, beliefs, habits and patterns. The conscious mind reacts to the environment, using the information that is stored in the subconscious. The conscious mind serves as short-term memory, while the subconscious holds all memories including consciously "forgotten" or repressed memories.

A good analogy for the mind is that of an iceberg (see figure 2), which has a small amount showing above water and a much larger part "hidden" below the water. Our conscious mind (the part of the iceberg above water) makes up only a small fraction of our mind (roughly 10%) and our subconscious comprises the vast majority (that huge part of the iceberg that is under water).

The conscious mind is the seat of rational and analytical thinking. It holds our ability to analyze problems and solve them in a rational way.

Another notion associated with the conscious mind is willpower (i.e. the conscious control over what we do). We use willpower when we consciously try to make ourselves do (or not do) something. For instance, "I'm

44

not going to bite my nails now" or "I'm not going to eat that donut".

Unfortunately, the conscious mind is weak and is easily swayed. Often times, when we are upset, angry or not at our full potential, we do things that are not rational, and our willpower is affected. We usually come to regret those decisions later, when we return to a more normal state. Similarly, you probably noticed that, when feeling tired or hungry, your reasoning is not as efficient and your willpower not as strong.

The vast majority of the power resides in the part of the mind "under the water line": the subconscious. It encompasses memories, habits (good and bad), emotions, feelings and thoughts that are outside of our conscious awareness.

Whenever there is a conflict between the conscious and the subconscious, the subconscious will always win in the end. The subconscious controls us in ways that are beyond our awareness. This is the reason why one can easily accept an idea intellectually (e.g. smoking is bad for me) but somehow do the exact opposite (habits and emotions reinforce the desire to smoke).

The "waterline" (the boundary between the conscious and subconscious minds) is known as the Conscious Critical Faculty (CCF). The CCF will be described in more detail later in this chapter.

◆

Figure 2 illustrates the iceberg analogy.

Introduction to hypnotherapy

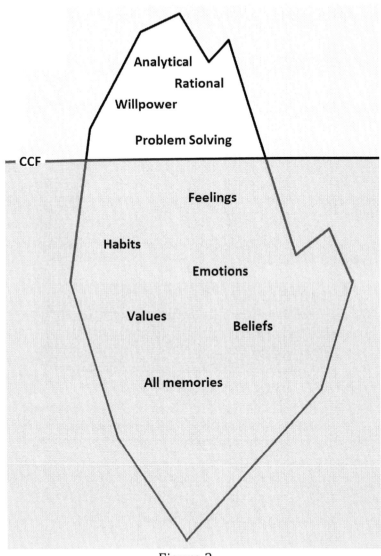

Figure 2

HOW IS HYPNOTHERAPY DIFFERENT FROM CONVENTIONAL THERAPY?

Unlike conventional therapies, which deal mainly with the conscious mind, hypnotherapy deals with the subconscious mind (which is not easily accessible in the normal way) in order to help release old patterns and "reprogram" the mind. The hypnotherapist achieves this by bypassing the conscious mind, and gaining access to the subconscious mind, where therapy takes place. This therapy can be based on positive suggestions or it can be of a more analytical nature (where the root cause of an issue is sought).

Because hypnotherapy deals directly with the subconscious, it usually provides much faster results than other therapeutic methods that work at the conscious level only. Specifically, hypnotherapy allows us to go where we need to operate in the subconscious so that adjustment can be made.

To continue with our earlier analogy, hypnotherapy allows us easier access to the part of the iceberg that was submerged.

CONSCIOUS CRITICAL FACULTY

The Conscious Critical Faculty (CCF) can be seen as the interface between the conscious mind and the subconscious mind. It constantly checks all sensory inputs and decides to accept or reject ideas based on past experiences. It tends to reject any suggestions that have not been accepted as "valid" thus far.

Introduction to hypnotherapy

If new suggestions do not agree with existing perception, they will be ignored or rejected. But if they do agree, they will be allowed through, thereby compounding the original perception and giving it power. For instance, once a child is told often enough that he is stupid (or ugly, fat, shy, short-tempered, stubborn or whatever), the CCF retains over time information confirming this "fact", but will tend to reject evidence to the contrary. This is true for both positive and negative attributes.

To make lasting changes in an individual, one needs to get "below" the CCF. The skilled hypnotherapist employs hypnosis to bypass the CCF and "implant" new ideas beneath it, in the subconscious mind. Once implanted, these suggestions will be acted upon, and will remain in place (as long as there are no conflicting beliefs) since the CCF will "protect" them from being changed again.

◆

It's important to note that the CCF's ability to question is diminished but not completely eliminated under hypnosis. There is a built-in safety feature. It's observing, ready to spring into action if necessary, for example if something is suggested which is against a client's morals or self-preservation mechanism. This is why hypnotherapy is very safe and will be most beneficial for those people who truly want to change. Now, if this is the case and change is not achieved as expressed, then it's possible that further investigation is required to uncover subconscious blocks to success.

SELECTIVE THINKING

Selective thinking is an increased mental involvement and a focused state of attention on the idea being presented. Paradoxically, selective thinking is both a way into and an effect of being in hypnosis. This is because the increased ability to hold an exclusive focus makes it easier to communicate effectively with the subconscious mind.

The "deeper" the subject goes into a trance state, the more effective selective thinking becomes. It's the combination of this focused attention with the CCF being bypassed and a relaxed state that contributes to a good therapy.

LEVELS OF TRANCE

There are different levels of trance, or depth of hypnosis. Depending on the type of therapy, the hypnotist will induce an appropriate level of hypnosis (from light to deep trance states).

The following describes commonly accepted levels of trance. However, keep in mind that this breakdown is somewhat arbitrary. In reality, the depth of trance is a continuum. The classifications below are only indicative and one moves *progressively* deeper as opposed to jumping from one level to the next.

Introduction to hypnotherapy

Light trance

The first level is a light trance. As we discussed in the introduction to this chapter, it is a state that we all enter naturally in our day-to-day life. It is commonly referred to as daydreaming.

For instance, while driving, your mind sometimes wanders and you may reach your destination without remembering some of the details of your journey. Another example of light trance is when you are engrossed in a good conversation with a friend and lose track of time and of what's happening around you; or when you are absorbed in a good book or movie.

While in this state, you will notice that your body is more relaxed, your breathing steadier and your attention more focused.

This level of trance can be induced by the hypnotist and is usually appropriate for simple suggestion therapy, NLP (Neuro-Linguistic Programming) and for therapies using metaphors and guided imagery.

The type of therapies that can be accomplished at this level include some habit control, self-esteem issues, stress, anxiety and some irrational fears and phobias (though some of the above may require more thorough work and therefore a deeper level).

Somnambulism

The next level is called "somnambulism". In its most common definition, somnambulism often designates a sleep disorder usually referred to as "sleepwalking".

In the context of hypnosis, there is, of course, no sleeping or walking involved, and it is just a label for a particular level of trance.

50

This is the level used by stage hypnotists and the level required by therapists for issues where a light trance is not sufficient.

This level of trance is the one used by most hypnotherapists. Some describe it as a state of blank nothingness during which suggestions are naturally accepted.

This level is perfect for:

- habit breaking (nail biting, smoking, etc.)
- psycho-somatic issues (physical ailments for which no medical issue is found)
- regression therapy (see chapter 7)
- accessing repressed memories

This state is usually strong enough for anesthesia in minor medical procedures such as tooth fillings or extractions.

Coma state or Esdaile state

The so-called "coma" state is not as ominous as it sounds. Sometimes also called the Esdaile state, it is a very deep level of trance, lower than somnambulism and is deep enough to perform major surgeries. Indeed, this is the level at which James Esdaile conducted amputations and other major procedures in Calcutta in the mid-1800s.

Individuals in this state experience feelings of bliss and euphoria. The breathing slows down and the subject is usually motionless and unable to speak (unlike light trance or somnambulism). It is a very enjoyable experience for clients. So much so, that it is usually more difficult to emerge them from this state.

Introduction to hypnotherapy

Sichort State

There is yet another – little known – level of trance, deeper than the Esdaile state: the Sichort state. In this state, the conscious mind completely gets out of the way, enabling the subconscious to come to the forefront.

It is sometimes described as a state of self-healing, in which miraculously fast healing has been reported to take place. Not everybody can reach this depth.

Note that the word "miracles" is used in its common meaning here and not as in *A Course in Miracles*. Please see the chapter "A Glimpse of Home?" in part 3 for a detailed coverage of deep trance states and how they relate to our true Self.

THE ROLE OF THE THERAPIST

The power of healing is not in the therapist but in the client. The therapist's role is to help clients unlock the power of their own mind and use their own resources to achieve the resolution of their issues. So, the therapist is merely a guide along their therapeutic journey. He's the Sherpa who will guide them to the top of the mountain, but will not drag them by force, nor carry their backpack for them. Therapy is definitely a collaborative endeavor.

It would be unfair to consider the therapist an all-knowing guru who has magical powers to cure. Yes, the therapist is trained and knowledgeable in techniques for positive change. But, like any profession, the effectiveness of his work comes from the way he practices his trade.

Looking at it in the context of *A Course in Miracles*, if coming from the ego's point of view, the therapy is unlikely to provide the results desired, but by working with the Holy Spirit "by his side", the therapist will be inspired to do the most loving thing for his clients.

One thing to keep in mind is that therapists are here in the illusion too. This means that we still have forgiveness lessons to learn as well. The Psychotherapy Pamphlet (an addendum to the Course) states: "The therapist sees in the patient all that he has not forgiven in himself, and is thus given another chance to look at it, open it to re-evaluation and forgive it."

So the client (or anybody else for that matter) is really a projection of the therapist's (perceived) sins and guilt. True healing can occur when the therapist realizes that fact and forgives himself.

We can see sickness as a form of lack of forgiveness. The internal conflict we all experience between ourselves and the perceived God (the ego's God) is manifested onto our body in the form of illness. So, the therapeutic encounter benefits the therapist as much as the client in that it is an opportunity for the therapist to see in someone else what he's afraid of seeing within himself. Forgiving his client (and thereby himself) is the true form of healing.

Important Note

It's important to note that, since hypnotherapy happens in the world we perceive, it is part of the illusion too (as is *A Course in Miracles* itself). Again, the techniques described should not be construed as a "cure" but as a means to an end. As we will see, the ego always strives to come up with new ways and techniques to "fix" our lives and make the "dream" more bearable. This book does not fit in this context. It

Introduction to hypnotherapy

recognizes that only through right-minded choices can the ego be undone. Therefore, the techniques described here are but a tool to help you practice the teachings of the Course, and not a solution in and of itself.

That being said, hypnotherapy (and psychotherapy) can be very useful within the illusion, in order to release past traumas that are impeding an individual's progress. For instance, if someone was abused as a child and the memory of that abuse was repressed, it is beneficial to use hypno-therapeutic techniques to uncover these memories so the person can release the "bottled up" emotions and forgive those involved (and themselves, of course).

CHAPTER SIX
-
HYPNOSIS MYTHS DEBUNKED

As discussed previously, hypnosis is a widely misunderstood phenomenon. Fueled by over-dramatic stage hypnotists and misleading movies, a large portion of the general public has developed an irrational fear of hypnosis. They picture themselves being made to quack like a duck or rob a bank under the spell of an evil hypnotist.

The reality is, of course, very different. As described in the previous section, hypnosis is a very natural state and is perfectly safe, whether it be under the guidance of a professional hypnotherapist or in a self-hypnosis session.

But, even though hypnotherapy is becoming increasingly popular and is gaining respect as a complementary therapy, it still suffers from a stigma due to fear and misconceptions. Below are some of the most common myths about hypnosis and an explanation of why they are unfounded.

Hypnosis myths debunked

Myth # 1
If you can be hypnotized, you have a "weak" mind

A very common myth is that only the feeble-minded can be hypnotized. This stems from the belief that the subject will be under the power of the hypnotist and do his bidding. Therefore, it is assumed that only the most gullible could fall for this.

The opposite is actually true. Hypnosis is a focused state of attention. So, the more the client is able to remain focused, the better hypnotic subject he will be. Therefore, a strong mind can better achieve the focus required for good levels of trance.

The only people who are not easily hypnotizable are people who are mentally challenged as they will lack the ability to focus. There are also people that should not be hypnotized such as those who are schizophrenic or delusional.

Some people go under hypnosis easier than others. Depending on the personality type of the client, the skilled hypnotist will adapt his approach to match the client's specificities and induce the appropriate level of hypnosis.

More than any inherent characteristic of the client, rapport and trust in the hypnotist is probably the most critical factor in ensuring a good level of hypnosis, since without trust, there will be resistance.

Also, there needs to be a willingness to be hypnotized and, in the context of therapy, a true desire to get better. Often, a hidden resistance is what gets in the way of a person achieving a good level of hypnosis.

Hypnotic Spirituality

Myth # 2
The hypnotist will have complete power over me and make me reveal secrets or do things against my will.

Another common myth is that the hypnotized subject will be made to do things they would not want to do or tell closely-held secrets they don't want to reveal. This, most likely, comes from the influence of stage hypnotists.

People who hold this belief have typically seen a stage hypnosis show, where people are made to do silly things on stage. One thing to realize is that the people on stage volunteered to be there. Usually, they are the most uninhibited amongst the crowd who love (sometimes secretly) to make a spectacle of themselves and be the center of attention, but ordinarily refrain from it due to social pressure.

On stage, under the "spell" of the hypnotist, they will go along with suggestions. After all, "it's not my fault I quacked like a duck; the hypnotist *made me* do it", they will claim.

It is crucial to understand that you remain in control while under hypnosis, and your subconscious mind remains vigilant to protect you. It will not allow anything that could damage you or is against your morals.

As an illustration of this, I remember attending a stage hypnosis show some years ago. The lady on stage was a stage hypnotist's delight. She was following his "commands" to the letter without hesitation and was extremely entertaining. Until the hypnotist asked her to dance and she did not follow the instructions. The hypnotist doubled his efforts and suggestions but she just stood there. A little embarrassed, he brought her out

57

Hypnosis myths debunked

of hypnosis and sent her back to her seat. I had a suspicion as to why this suggestion did not work when all previous ones worked so well. So, I caught up with her after the show and chatted with her a bit. It turns out my suspicion was right. She was a devout fundamentalist Christian from a denomination where dancing is severely frowned upon and considered a sin. So, even though this lady was under hypnosis, she would only go along with the suggestions that she found acceptable and did not violate her innate morals.

As for revealing secrets, the same principle applies. You will only reveal what is in your own best interest. In a therapeutic setting, clients wish to overcome an issue. They know it is in their best interest to reveal all relevant information. They know the therapist is bound by an oath of privacy and that, unlike friends and relatives, they probably won't see him again outside the consulting room.

They also know that the therapist wants the best outcome for them, so the subconscious will go along and the person may reveal things that they had never told anyone before. However, the hypnotist could not *force* them to reveal things verbally; it is the client's choice.

Myth # 3
You can be hypnotized against your will

Some people have the misconception that they can be hypnotized against their will. However, this is not the case. The collaboration of the client is required to create a good level of hypnosis. If the subject wants to resist, he can. Of course, people who come to see a hypnotherapist have a real desire to solve some issue. After all, they are

Hypnotic Spirituality

spending time and money, so it would not make sense for them to resist.

As long as the person has the desire to be hypnotized, they can be. But, once again, the hypnotist cannot *force* them to. In reality, as Charles Tebbetts (a prominent and influential hypnotherapist) taught, all hypnosis is self-hypnosis and the power is in the mind of the person being hypnotized. The therapist is merely a guide through the process.

Myth # 4
I didn't get hypnotized, I heard every word!

Another commonly heard statement is "I didn't get hypnotized, I heard every word!" This comes from the mistaken belief that one is asleep while in hypnosis. As we discussed earlier, the confusion stems from the fact that the word hypnosis comes from the Greek root *hypnos,* which means sleep. James Braid, who coined the term "hypnosis", later tried to change it, but the word had become so widely adopted that he was unable to do so.

Far from being asleep, the attention of the hypnotized subject is actually more focused on something specific. They are still aware of what is happening around them, but only peripherally. It is similar to when you are concentrating on a detailed task and your eyes are focused on that task, but you still perceive things in your peripheral vision, and would react to it if you perceived a danger coming from the side.

Similarly, under hypnosis, you are still aware of your surroundings, but they fade away as you focus on the topic of the hypnotherapy session. However, if a danger

Hypnosis myths debunked

were perceived (such as someone yelling "fire!"), you would immediately be able to react to it and snap out of hypnosis.

Once again, there's no standard "feeling" of hypnosis and everyone reacts slightly differently. Some people's conscious mind may drift off to some pleasant thought or other preoccupation. By letting their mind wander, these people may "miss" consciously what the hypnotist is saying. And that's OK since the hypnotherapy is directed at the subconscious mind. The session will be no less effective as the subconscious will absorb the suggestions whether the conscious mind is paying attention or not.

Some other people's conscious mind will remain tuned to the hypnotist's voice and hear every word. Some others may drift in and out and only remember parts of the session.

All these reactions are normal, and since the therapist talks to the subconscious, the therapy will be just as successful whether the client "hears" every word of the session or not.

Myth # 5
You can remain permanently stuck in hypnosis

We saw that hypnosis is a natural phenomenon that we all experience throughout our daily lives. Whether it is spontaneous or induced by a hypnotist (or a self-hypnosis recording), it is a safe and natural state. As such, there's no risk of remaining "stuck" in hypnosis, just like there's no risk of being "stuck" awake or asleep.

There are no reported cases of anyone becoming stuck in hypnosis. Some people may take a little longer

Hypnotic Spirituality

than others to emerge from trance, depending on the depth of the trance and their propensity to be hypnotized, but they always emerge.

In the (very unlikely) scenario where a hypnotist would die or pass out while his client is in hypnosis, the hypnotized subject would either drift into sleep and eventually wake up normally after the nap, or they would gradually realize that something is wrong due to the lack of input from the hypnotist and emerge from hypnosis naturally.

This was actually scientifically researched. In a study titled "Inadvertent termination of hypnosis with hypnotized and simulating subjects", published in the *International Journal of Clinical and Experimental Hypnosis*, Orne & Evans demonstrated that, if subjects under hypnosis are left by themselves, they always naturally emerge on their own.

Myth # 6
I'll become dependent on the hypnotist.

This myth is related to the belief that the hypnotist has full power and control over his client, which we know is not the case. If anything, therapy will usually help clients become more self-reliant and independent.

That being said, there are some clients, particularly those with low self-esteem, who will develop a sort of addiction to the therapy itself. This is a form of resistance and will be discussed later in this book. Such clients may have identified so much with their "condition" that they fear losing their identity if they were to no longer suffer from their "issue". As a result, they subconsciously sabotage their progress. As long as

Hypnosis myths debunked

they are in therapy, they still have their issue and therefore are still themselves. This phenomenon is not related to hypnosis however. It is found by psychotherapists, CBT practitioners, NLP practitioners and any counselor. The skilled therapist will detect this situation and handle it appropriately.

Myth # 7
I won't remember anything that happened when I was hypnotized

As discussed earlier, one remains aware while under hypnosis. Some people's conscious mind may wander a bit during the session and they may only remember parts of it. And that's all right.

During the session, the therapist addresses the subconscious mind. So, it does not matter what the conscious mind does and whether or not it remembers the contents of the session. The subconscious will absorb and remember, and that's what really matters.

Again, there's no right or wrong way to experience hypnosis. It is best to just go with what feels natural, not trying to remember everything, and at the same time not trying to forget the session either.

62

CHAPTER SEVEN

-

METHODS OF HYPNOTHERAPY

Hypnotherapy is an expansive field incorporating a wide variety of techniques. The skilled therapist will have many of these techniques at his disposal and will employ those most suited to his client's needs and personality type. Broadly speaking, hypnotherapy techniques can be separated into two main types: suggestion and analytical. An overview of the main techniques in each category follows. We will apply a lot of these techniques to the Course's teachings in part 3.

SUGGESTION THERAPY

Suggestion therapy is probably the best known form of hypnotherapy. It is also the most commonly practiced by therapists since other forms (such as analytical styles) require more advanced training and practice.

POSITIVE SUGGESTIONS

After a good level of hypnosis is reached, positive suggestions are offered to the subconscious mind to bring about the desired changes.

Methods of hypnotherapy

It's important to emphasize the keyword "suggestion" as the therapy indeed merely suggests (it does not order or command) to the subconscious that a new behavior is more appropriate for the well-being of the client.

As long as there is no conflict with the individual's moral or ethical beliefs (or no deeper rooter issues involved), the suggestions will be accepted and acted upon by the subconscious. The new behavior will therefore become unconscious, which means it will not require willpower in order to be effected.

This is one of the techniques employed in this book to help you apply Course principles at a subconscious level. These will be covered in Part 3.

Note

Suggestion therapy may not be sufficient for full resolution of some issues. Sometimes, a problem has its roots in a past event or trauma. In this case, uncovering techniques (such as parts therapy or regression styles of therapy) may be required. These methods will be described in more details later in this chapter.

Jill's story

Jill had a nail biting habit. She was 32, healthy both physically and emotionally, with a successful career in the IT industry. She showed me her hands and chewed-up nails and asked if I could help her stop this habit. She had tried to control her biting with willpower but had been unable to. She longed to have healthy, manicured nails. This had become especially important for her as her wedding day was only a few months away, and she really wanted to have lovely hands for this occasion. I used a set of suggestions to help her gain conscious

Hypnotic Spirituality

awareness of when she was bringing her hands to her mouth in order to bite them and then to automatically refrain from doing so, replacing her biting urge with her taking a deep, relaxing breath of fresh air. I also used a great deal of positive imagery and suggestions to help her picture herself with beautiful long nails and all her wedding guests commenting how beautiful her nails were. With the strong motivation that Jill possessed, the suggestions offered were readily accepted and she reported later that she had beautiful manicured nails on her special day.

METAPHORS

Metaphors are, in my opinion, one of the most useful techniques in the hypnotherapist's toolbox. They are actually not unique to hypnotherapy. They are used commonly by psychotherapists and NLP practitioners. But, I believe using metaphors under hypnosis makes them a lot more powerful, since the mind is more able to focus, the conscious critical faculty is bypassed, and the associations of the metaphor can take root at the subconscious level instead of the conscious level.

At a basic level, a metaphor is a tool to help express and understand one thing in terms of another. The smallest metaphor is a symbol where a word or image is used to represent a specific characteristic.

In a therapeutic context, metaphors are used to help people understand and accept complex concepts by using a story that is easier to comprehend and resonates with the individual's personal background. In so doing, the subconscious can draw parallels and leverage the internal resources required to effect the desired change.

Methods of hypnotherapy

The story is written in a way that it symbolizes the issue the client is suffering from. As the story comes to a successful resolution, so does the client's problem indirectly. Even though the plot and characters of the story are different from the real problem, the underlying patterns and structure are the same. The subconscious associates with the characters and the story (and its happy conclusion) and it becomes, in a way, part of the client's reality.

Metaphors do not have to be realistic. They are often over-dramatic and can include fantasy elements and events that could not happen in the real world. In a way, they are made even more effective by such elements, since they stimulate the imagination.

Often, the conclusion of the story is not expressly stated, leaving the client to draw their own conclusion and the subconscious to find a solution accordingly.

A famous example is given by Milton Erickson who, when counseling a couple with sexual issues, used a food metaphor. The husband was prone to go straight for the main course, while the wife enjoyed spending time sampling appetizers first. He suggested they plan a full 5-course dinner together which, for reasons that were not obvious to them, resulted in a drastic improvement of their sex life.

I use metaphors heavily in my work and recommend you do the same if you write self-hypnosis scripts. In part 3, I will offer example metaphors to enable easier acceptance the principles of the Course. But these are just examples. Metaphors are more powerful when tailored to the particular individual, leveraging his own personal or cultural idiosyncrasies. Feel free to adapt the examples I give to your own situation or use them as inspiration to come up with new ones.

66

I should also point out that the Course is full of metaphors since the concepts it refers to cannot really be described in words or directly understood by us. We should therefore be very careful when reading it not to take the words literally. Anything that would seem to indicate any element of duality is certainly a metaphor and should be treated as such.

ANALYTICAL THERAPY

Analytical hypnotherapy techniques take many forms, the majority of which involve the client speaking to the therapist while in hypnosis. Because hypnosis allows clients access to subconscious processes, these methods can be highly successful at uncovering the root cause of certain issues. A description of the main analytical hypnotherapy techniques can be found below.

PARTS THERAPY

We all experience internal conflicts. A part of us pulls in one direction and another part in a different direction. These conflicts are normal to some extent, but for some people, those parts are more defined and influence their behavior significantly (and often negatively).

Parts therapy aims to identify, under hypnosis, the different parts and have them express their respective agenda and reasons for the behavior they prescribe. We then come up with an agreement between the parts that will be in the best interest of the client.

I will cover this subject in a lot more details and discuss how you can apply it to your spiritual practice in the chapter "A part of me" in Part 3.

Methods of hypnotherapy

REGRESSION THERAPY

Sometimes, suggestion therapy is not enough. This is the case when the issue or symptoms are the result of an underlying cause - a past event, usually traumatic at the time, and often repressed. Trying to use only suggestion therapy in this case would be akin to using a Band-Aid for a deep wound or just patching up a big crack in the wall which indicates a foundation issue; it may hide the problem temporarily, but the crack (or a more serious problem) is bound to come back as the root cause of the problem was not addressed.

Regression therapy enables the client to access past memories (including those that have been repressed and are not consciously accessible). This allows the therapist to assist the client in finding the root cause of a problem, leading to the release of the associated issue.

There are two main styles of regression:

- **Directed regression**: in this style, the therapist guides the client back in time to find the Initial Sensitizing Event (ISE). This approach is effective when there is a clear symptom that has an ISE which can be uncovered. It is not appropriate when there are a variety of symptoms or when it's not clear what specific issues need to be resolved. Common methodologies of this style are:
  - o Regression to Cause
  - o Time Track therapy

- **Non-directed regression**: this style utilizes the technique known as free association and is the most holistic in its approach.

68

Regression to Cause

The subconscious mind stores memories and information related to all events that we have ever experienced. Some of these events and the emotions attached to them were traumatic and too difficult to handle at the time, especially when they were experienced as a child. So, the feelings and emotions attached to these events (and often the actual memories themselves) end up being repressed and hidden in the depths of the subconscious, and are not accessible to the conscious mind. These repressed memories often "leak" out of the subconscious as symptoms in adult life.

Whatever the cause, the fact is that the event happened and cannot be changed. But what can be changed is the emotional response to the event. By bringing the memory and its associated emotions into the conscious mind (what is known as revivification), examining it in detail with an adult's knowledge and resources, and rationalizing it, the event typically loses its power, and the negative effects and unwanted symptoms disappear.

The "Affect Bridge" is a common method of regression to cause. Using this technique, the client focuses as vividly as possible on the last time he experienced his symptoms (for instance a feeling of panic or fear). Once connected with the feelings and emotions related to his issue, he is then guided back to an earlier time when he felt that way; and then an earlier and earlier time until he reaches the very first time he experienced this emotional response (the ISE). The repeated revivification of this particular event results in lessening and eventual clearing of the emotional trauma and its related symptoms.

69

Methods of hypnotherapy

Note that the revivification of the event can be quite emotional and may be accompanied by tears and, in some cases, body gesticulations (as the client goes through what is termed an abreaction). Though, on the surface, it may appear cruel to have to relive those past events, this is actually very therapeutic as the client becomes less and less affected by the event with each repetition until it becomes completely insignificant to him. Once again, the event has happened and nothing can be done to change this fact. However, the emotional reaction to the event (and its psychological and physical effects) can be changed and this is exactly what this type of therapy is all about.

Here's an example that will illustrate the type of associations made by the subconscious and how they can result in unexpected effects.

Julia's story

Food allergies are fairly common and can often be traced by doctors to some chemical intolerance. What made Julia's allergy interesting was that doctors could not find any medical reason why she would be allergic to cherries. She loved food and ate every type of fruit, but for some reason, if she ate a cherry, she would break out in hives and start having difficulty breathing, Even being near them caused her to feel uncomfortable.

I used an age-regression method to help Julia trace back the origin of her allergy. I asked her to go progressively further back in time to instances where she was subjected to this cherry allergy. After a few inconsequential incidents, Julia started describing a memory that her conscious mind had forgotten: she was a young child (maybe 3 or 4) and was standing in her backyard. She recounted seeing her parents arguing violently, her father even hitting her mother at one point. There was a cherry tree in the backyard, and since this was early summer, ripe cherries were scattered on the ground. Julia's subconscious mind had made an association between what is obviously a traumatic experience for a young child and the cherries. In an effort to "protect" Julia from similar traumas, her subconscious tried its hardest to keep her away from cherries. The uncomfortable feeling around them and reaction when eaten was an attempt by her subconscious to prevent future interaction with cherries. This is, of course, an irrational train of thought, but such is the way of the subconscious. Through the revivification of the event, combined with her more rational adult awareness, her fear and allergy of cherries was gone.

TIME-TRACK THERAPY

Time-track therapy allows the client to go back in their mind to a past event and take with them resources (such as their now-adult understanding or newfound knowledge) that they were not in possession of at the time of the event. The therapist guides the client to the event and assists him in using these resources to gain insight and a new perspective with regards to the situation and what would have been required by them to avoid trauma. Time-track therapy is sometimes also used to take the client into the future (a form of future pacing) to experience what their upcoming life will be like without the issue they are currently suffering from.

Methods of hypnotherapy

This form of therapy is sometimes used in combination with regression and parts therapy.

NON-DIRECTED REGRESSION THERAPY

In this style of regression, the therapist does not guide the client in any specific way or to any specific event, but lets the client's mind jump from one memory to another freely. Non-directed regression is usually referred to as hypno-analysis or hypno-psychotherapy and utilizes the technique of free association (where the subconscious automatically goes to memories that are relevant to the client's issues).

Most hypnotherapists refer to this technique as "the cream" of all techniques. This approach is very effective at uncovering and resolving a wide range of issues. Due to its holistic nature, it is possible for a client to resolve a whole host of issues during the course of therapy, even those that he may not have been aware of.

Free Association

Free association is a technique not unique to hypnotherapy; it is also used in standard talk therapy (psycho-analysis) and was popularized by Sigmund Freud. It involves letting the client say whatever comes into his mind. The memories recalled are not linear, but they follow an "unconscious thread" which leads to insights and internal conflict resolution.

When conducted under hypnosis, this method becomes even more effective (it usually only takes 8-12 sessions) since the client has access to memories that may not be consciously available, and the focused state of attention allows them to concentrate more easily. Moreover, the relaxed feeling procured by hypnosis helps the client let go and feel more comfortable in sharing memories that may otherwise be held back out of embarrassment.

◆

Here's an outline of a typical hypno-analysis session.

Once in hypnosis, the therapist guides the client back in time to the early years of his life and asks him to find himself in a memory of something that happened at some point and to verbalize that experience, without analyzing it or questioning it in any way. Then, without trying to make any connection at all in the conscious mind, the client allows his mind to drift to the next experience, which he once again recounts to the therapist, before moving on to the next one, and so on. It's that simple...but highly effective!

The client is actually recounting psychological experiences, not just memories. The difference between a memory and a psychological experience is that the former usually just includes the physical details of an event, while the latter accesses the emotional responses to that event as well. All that is required for the client is to say whatever comes to mind, without trying to analyze it. If the work is to be effective, the client must be sure to say the very first thought each time, regardless of how apparently unimportant, unrelated or potentially embarrassing the memory may be.

The rationale behind this process is that we are searching for unfinished "childhood business", which can be minor (or maybe not so minor). Some of what surfaces during analysis are memories of situations which bothered the client as a child, some to a degree where either the memory or the emotion or both were simply "swept under the carpet", until therapy allowed them to surface and be dealt with. By expressing the original emotions that had been repressed and "forgotten", clients are usually relieved of their symptoms (a process known as catharsis).

In addition to the removal of anxiety and other emotional states associated with events from the past, this technique has some positive "side effects", such as increased self-confidence and a lowering of stress levels.

PAST LIFE REGRESSION

The notion of past lives is a controversial topic. A lot of people are convinced you only get "one go 'round", and that you'd better make the most of it. They consider the concept of multiple lives a delusion. Others believe that what we call "our life" is but one incarnation, and that we keep coming back into the world and (hopefully) make spiritual progress each time until we reach *Nirvana* (or whatever you want to call it). Since you are reading a book on how to speed up your spiritual growth, I will assume that you are spiritual and believe in re-incarnation (or are at least open to the possibility).

Past Life Regression (PLR) allows someone to re-experience sections of former lives. The clients who come to see a hypnotherapist for past life regression can have different motives. Some want to experience it out of curiosity. Others have feelings that they lived in a particular era and want to go check if they are right. Yet others suffer from a condition in this life which they believe could have originated in a previous life, and they want to explore that possibility and hopefully resolve the issue. For the latter, the process is similar to the age regression technique described earlier, except the regression goes back further through time to a former life.

◆

A typical Past Life Regression session starts with inducing a fairly deep state of hypnosis. This induction is usually tailored to prepare the mind to go back to past memories. The therapist may use a set of questions to elicit descriptions of surroundings and events in a past lifetime. The client describes where they are, what they are doing, who they are with, etc. The memories are usually very vivid, detailed and realistic.

Some people recognize present-day friends and family members in different roles in their past lives. Sometimes they may even be married to the same person, but the husband and wife roles may be reversed. People may find themselves to be a different gender, race, nationality, etc.; sometimes one that they despise today. This type of experience is usually very positive as it demonstrates to people that their current self is only a temporary vehicle, and next time around, they could just as easily be in the other group that they so hate. People are usually more open-minded after such an experience.

It is also often found that people who were the perpetrators of some crime or abuse are victims of similar situations in this life (or vice-versa).

Finally, it is not uncommon for clients to witness their own death in a previous life. This experience is usually

Methods of hypnotherapy

very fulfilling as the individual realizes that death is but a milestone and not the end; this helps many carrying on living without fear of death.

Bill's story

Bill had quite an unusual problem. He had a fear of sand. The thought of going to the beach was horrifying to him and, as far as he could remember, he had always been uncomfortable on or near sand. We started with some standard age-regression. I expected to find a typical childhood memory where a bully had thrown sand in his face, or perhaps some repressed memory of child abuse on a sand dune. But, there was none of that. Bill's childhood was, by all accounts, a happy one and no negative association to sand (even far-fetched) was revealed.

I knew Bill was spiritual and believed in re-incarnation so I suggested we tried a Past Life Regression and he accepted. Bill found himself as a Bedouin in 18th century Arabia. He described in details the garments he was wearing and his life as a Bedouin. He recounted that, one day, he and his brother had ventured alone in the desert and got caught in a sand storm. Despite being used to this type of conditions, the storm was so strong that they were fighting for their lives. Bill made it out alive, but tragically, his brother did not. Tears were rolling down his face as he told the story and it was obvious that the experience felt very real to him. Bill said he felt tremendous guilt over not being able to save his brother's life. He apparently had carried this guilt and its association to sand into his current life.

76

Now that the memory had been brought into conscious awareness, he stated that he was feeling better already and was not excluding approaching sand again. A couple of months later, I received a postcard from Bill from a beach resort with a simple "Thank you!" written on it.

I leave it for you to decide whether the events Bill experienced were indeed part of a past life or a fantasy in his mind. What matters to me, as a therapist, is that Bill believed in it and felt better as a result of it.

In the chapter "Whose life is it anyway?" in part 3, we examine how past life regression can be applied to spiritual paths.

CHAPTER EIGHT
-
A GUIDE TO SELF-HYPNOSIS

If you cannot work with a hypnotherapist (either because there is not a suitable one in your area or you cannot afford to do so) or download one of our audio programs, you can still benefit from the techniques taught in this book by putting together your own self-hypnosis sessions. Relax...it's not as hard as it sounds. This chapter will teach you how to write self-hypnosis scripts and prepare you for the sessions.

I recommend you read all the previous chapters in this section for background information on hypnosis before studying this chapter.

STRUCTURE

A typical self-hypnosis session has the following basic structure:

- **Induction**: this is where you will start going into hypnosis. There are a multitude of induction scripts available online. A progressive relaxation script is a classic that works well for most people. A sample of

A guide to self-hypnosis

such a script is given in Appendix A but feel free to write your own.

- **Deepener**: as its name indicates, the deepener increases the depth of hypnosis. There are many different types but often involves some kind of counting down (for instance going down steps one at a time). You should now be in a state deep enough for therapeutic work. A sample deepener is given in Appendix A.

- **Therapy**: now that you have reached a good level of hypnosis, you can start to work on the specific purpose of the session. For self-hypnosis, you will be using suggestion therapy, since parts therapy, regression and hypno-analysis are difficult to do on one's own and requires more advanced hypno-therapy training. You can use the ideas given in the various exercises of part 3 or come up with your own. The section below gives you tips on how to write good suggestions (this is known as a "script").

- **Emerging**: this part brings you out of hypnosis. It is fairly short and usually involves counting up slowly to progressively emerge. Appendix A gives a sample emerging script.

HOW TO WRITE GOOD SUGGESTION SCRIPTS

Suggestion scripts are not difficult to write but there are a few guidelines to follow to make them effective. Apply the following tips when you write your scripts:

Hypnotic Spirituality

- **Stay focused**. Always keep in mind the focus and purpose of your session. Avoid the temptation to try to cover too many topics in one session. You should be repetitive and come back to the same idea a few times using different phrasings. Be confident in your delivery.

- **Use the present tense**. Phrase your suggestions as if you had already achieved the goal. The best way to do this is to use the present tense. For instance, instead of saying "I will be more confident when speaking publicly", say "I am a confident public speaker".

- **Do not try.** Follow Yoda's wise advice: "Do or do not, there is no try". By using the word "try", you are already implying that you might fail. So, be confident that you will be successful and avoid any word that implies uncertainty.

- **Keep it simple**. Treat the subconscious as a child and write your scripts as if you were talking to one. Avoid complex or lengthy sentences and stay away from sophisticated words. Keep it clear, simple and to the point.

- **Stir the imagination**. Use powerful and exciting words. It's important to stir the imagination by using powerful adjectives to excite the subconscious and generate powerful feelings and a positive emotional impact. It is a good idea to stimulate the imagination by using images and symbols. Visualization is a powerful way to make a goal a reality, by imagining yourself already having accomplished that goal.

A guide to self-hypnosis

- **Keep it realistic.** Try to keep your suggestions realistic otherwise you risk the subconscious rejecting them outright. It is better to encourage your subconscious to make continuous progress than set an unachievable goal.

- **Use positive language.** Phrase your suggestions in a positive way. The subconscious does not understand negatives. For instance, if I ask you to NOT think of a pink elephant, what did you just think of? A pink elephant. So, keep your suggestions positive. For example, instead of saying "I will not eat junk food anymore", say "I always make healthy food choices".

USE OF METAPHORS

Metaphors are a very useful tool in hypnotherapy. For details on the principles of metaphors, please read the corresponding section in the "Methods of Hypnotherapy" chapter.

Here are a few tips to help you apply metaphors in your self-hypnosis scripts:

- Keep the stories easy to follow and in simple language.

- Use analogies that resonate with you. The metaphors will be more powerful if they relate to things you are familiar with or you are passionate about.

- Don't hesitate to make the stories over-dramatic and do not shy away from fantasies and symbolic imagery. Stimulating the imagination will make the metaphor more effective.

YOUR SELF-HYPNOSIS SESSION

Now that you have written your script, it's time to put it into practice. You can either have someone read it to you or you can record it and play it to yourself. I don't recommend trying to memorize the script and reciting it to yourself as the distraction of trying to remember the script will affect your ability to remain in hypnosis and benefit from the experience.

Find a quiet place where you will not be disturbed. Unplug the phone and keep pets and children away. You can either sit in a comfortable chair (with your legs uncrossed and your feet on the ground) or lie on a sofa or bed. It is also a good idea to play some soothing relaxing music in the background. Some people find the smell of incense relaxing as well; if you're one of them, go ahead and burn some incense.

Start by breathing slowly and deeply. This will start the relaxation. Make sure you build this breathing exercise into your induction script or allow enough time for it at the beginning of your recording.

Proceed with your recording, letting go, without worrying whether you are doing it right or wrong or if what you are feeling is normal. Remember there's no specific feeling of hypnosis that you are expected to

83

A guide to self-hypnosis

experience. So just go with it, let whatever happens happen and... enjoy the experience.

In order to be more effective, I recommend repeating sessions. One session on its own is usually not going to be truly effective. In order to avoid boredom, you can rotate your scripts instead of using the same one every day for an extended period of time.

PART 3
-
HYPNOTIC SPIRITUALITY

INTRODUCTION

This section comprises the essence of the book. In Part 1, we reviewed the main principles of *A Course in Miracles*. In Part 2, I gave you some general knowledge on hypnosis and hypnotherapy, so that the techniques described here will make sense. This section is where we bring it all together.

I believe that hypnotherapy has vast untapped potential. Until relatively recently, it had been considered (and still is in some areas) an arcane art, akin to witchcraft. Nowadays, more and more people are benefiting from hypnotherapy, and it is becoming mainstream to the point where one does not have to be embarrassed or ashamed of admitting to consulting a hypnotherapist. In fact, those who realize the power of hypnosis should consider themselves wise indeed.

As we discussed in part 2, the subconscious drives most of our emotions and habits, and can easily override (and undermine) our conscious efforts to change. By communicating with the subconscious mind, the hypnotherapist can assist a client in breaking bad habits and behaviors while establishing beneficial ones. This is an oversimplification of course, but for the purpose of this discussion, it is totally adequate.

This book's mission is to help you achieve a better understanding of *A Course in Miracles* at a deeper level of

Introduction

mind and therefore achieve faster progress in applying its principles. Most of us understand the Course's principles intellectually, but struggle to put them into practice and our progress is slow or short-lived; we easily slide back into old bad habits.

So, this section is comprised of a set of chapters each detailing how hypnosis and hypnotherapeutic techniques can help you with your spiritual quest. Throughout this section, I will outline practical step-by-step exercises and give examples of client sessions to illustrate the techniques. This should help design your own self-hypnosis scripts, or work with your chosen hypnotherapist to prepare sessions. If you choose the former option, the guide to self-hypnosis at the end of Part 2 should prove helpful.

CHAPTER NINE

-

AIN'T NO SACRIFICE... AT ALL

One of the biggest obstacles most people face in their quest for spiritual growth is a lack of motivation and a reluctance to abandon the world. It may sound odd at first that we could be lacking motivation to get back to "heaven", but many people are disinclined to give up an interesting and thrilling (albeit often painful) world for what they perceive as the boring state of homeostasis in heaven. Indeed, heaven is described in the Course as formless and changeless, and since we're used to the ups and downs of life and the drama attached to them, heaven seems awfully dull.

In reality, of course, this reluctance stems from fear: the fear of losing one's identity, and most importantly the fear of God's love. We will discuss fear in greater detail in Chapter 13, but it seems appropriate to dedicate this section's first chapter to motivation; otherwise, you may have little incentive to pursue the exercises discussed in later chapters. It's a little like the gym: we know we should go, but unless we have a strong drive, something that inspires us and motivates us, and some concrete goals we're striving for (be they

Ain't no sacrifice...at all

aesthetic or health-related), we're unlikely to lift those weights and run on that treadmill.

There are two main aspects to our lack of motivation. The first is the foolish notion that this world is "not that bad". You can address this by having an honest look at your life and the world at large. The second one is realizing what heaven might be like, and experiencing enough of a glimpse of it that you can imagine what it might *really* be like. At that point, the comparison between the two becomes obvious, and you can start to realize that you're not giving up anything in return for everything. You can then *truly* strive for heaven, as opposed to just paying lip service to it.

In this chapter, you will first see how hypnotherapy techniques can be used to raise your awareness of the world, and be more honest with yourself in its assessment. You will then learn how deep levels of hypnosis seem to take us into a state that approximates our heavenly state. You will also see how you can use these states to get a sense of what oneness may be like, thereby generating the motivation necessary to be more diligent with respect to putting Course principles into practice.

By working through the exercises outlined in this chapter, you will start to see that leaving this world is no sacrifice...at all.

HAVE AN HONEST LOOK AT IT

The way the Course portrays the world is pretty gruesome. It is described as "merciless indeed, unstable, cruel, unconcerned with you, quick to avenge and

Hypnotic Spirituality

pitiless with hate" (W129.2:3-6); a pretty grim picture indeed.

However, when we look at our lives, we convince ourselves that things aren't that bad. We might argue, "sure, it has its share of pains and frustrations, but look at those moments of happiness I experience occasionally; look at that pretty mountain scenery or that gorgeous star-lit sky; listen to this beautiful song". We go on and on rationalizing that everything is fine in the world and deny or bury its awfulness: the wars, murders, greed, intolerance, disasters, diseases and the constant pain inflicted by individuals or groups against each other. The Buddha summarized it perfectly when He said "life is suffering".

And this is not a new phenomenon; suffering has been a staple of human existence since the beginning of time. What hope is there really that things will suddenly get better, when we know that the world was designed specifically for this purpose: to allow us to feel like victims, thereby projecting our perceived sinfulness on someone or something else.

The "pleasures" we experience in life are usually ephemeral and only pleasurable when judged in relation to the usual suffering. Here's an analogy to illustrate the point: if you are locked up for life in a dark dungeon, you may be able to see out of the corner of your cell window, and occasionally catch a glimpse of the sky and a star shining. You may be awestruck by the star and marvel at its beauty, which may fill you with a relative sense of joy. However, it is to be short-lived, as you quickly realize you are shackled to the floor of a filthy jail, and here comes the warden for your daily beating session. Moreover, the pleasures are only "pleasurable" when compared to the pain. It's a little like the pleasure of

91

Ain't no sacrifice...at all

taking off shoes that are painfully tight and uncomfortable. Would you really want to purposely wear tight and uncomfortable shoes all day, just for the pleasure of taking them off at night? Yet, this is exactly what we are doing by arguing that life in the world is pleasurable.

This apparent pleasure comes from our inherent perceived weakness, our mistaken belief that we are vulnerable and subject to the whim of a merciless and fickle world. By forgetting our Christ nature, we accept the suffering as normal and relish every tiny bit of relative pleasure, when infinite pleasures are at our disposal. As the Course metaphorically asks us, why we would be satisfied with a crumb when we can have the whole banquet? Why would we limit ourselves to a drop of water when we can have the whole ocean?

By refusing to admit the awfulness of the world, seeking solace in it and clinging to crumbs of pleasure, we are, in effect, in denial. This form of denial is obviously unhealthy, and an honest assessment of the world is necessary before we can expect to make any progress. The Text and the Workbook keep warning us that looking for happiness in the world is a futile exercise, and invite us to truly face "our demons". Before you see peace, you need to acknowledge the horror. In other words, you must first face your guilt before you can choose love and you must realize the hatred in your mind before you will truly see the world. In order to do that, you must first look at your *choice* to be guilty before you can hope to be guiltless.

◆

Hypnotic Spirituality

So, how can hypnotherapy help us? Well, first of all, since our denial is unconscious, we can help bring it to the surface and into conscious awareness. I do not aim to remove those false beliefs, but to simply make you more conscious of them. A good analogy may be the client who consults a hypnotherapist regarding a bad habit they want to get rid of (for instance, they bite their nails). They are usually unaware consciously that they are doing it, and only see the results of their action (i.e. chewed up finger nails). A common hypnotherapeutic approach is to install a trigger that will make them aware of every time they bring their hand towards their mouth to chew their nails. Some dramatic imagery is sometimes used, such as having the client picture his hand growing out of proportion as he bring it up to his mouth to chew it. This technique brings conscious awareness of his behavior and can be enough for him stop biting his nails.

A similar approach can be used here, in which we install triggers that will bring to your awareness your mistaken belief of vulnerability and your denial of the awfulness of the world. By "catching" yourself when you deny the horrors of the world, the pains in your life and your ego-driven behaviors, you become more aware of them and start to acknowledge them for what they are.

The goal is not to only see doom and gloom and live a life of depression, but simply to have an honest and true view of your life and the world around you. We are also not aiming to remove all fun from life; nothing in the Course says you should not enjoy life, as it is a course at the level of thought and does not prescribe what to do and not to do in the world. We simply want to become aware of the underlying thoughts.

Ain't no sacrifice...at all

If you think the world and your life are great as they are, then maybe *A Course in Miracles* is not for you. But if you truly, deeply believed that, you would not even be in the world. So, it's a form a denial that may be holding your spiritual progress back. Note that this is normal and we all experience this denial to some extent. But by raising our awareness, we can progressively come to terms with what the world really is. This is what this section is all about.

 Here are some steps to get started along that path (either working with a hypnotist or using self-hypnosis):

1. Start by inducing a light to medium state of hypnosis
2. Let your mind drift to the memory of an event that you consider pleasurable
3. Replay that scene in your mind in vivid details
4. Examine the feelings and emotions associated with it
5. Perform an honest assessment of this event
   a. What was the source of the related joy?
   b. Was the joy lasting or only temporary?
   c. Was it sustained or followed by disillusionment?
   d. Was it at the expense of someone else?
   e. Was anybody excluded?
   f. Was any form of judgment subtly involved?
   g. Was the joy only relative (i.e. in comparison to tough times that preceded it or followed it)?
   h. What is the purpose of the "joyful" event? Ego or Holy Spirit?
6. Repeat this exercise for a few more pleasurable scenes

Hypnotic Spirituality

7. Now think of an upcoming event of everyday life that you are looking forward to
8. Picture yourself at the event being very present and aware of your feelings
9. Run through the questions on item 5.
10. Now picture a scene that is unpleasant
11. Be aware of the negative feelings involved
12. Be aware of the temptation to bury those feelings and to ignore them
13. Repeat for a few similar scenes
14. From now on, whenever you are (subconsciously) in denial of the awfulness of a situation and its negative aspects, this awareness will naturally come to your conscious mind
15. When acting from your ego (represented by feelings of anger, upset, depression, judgment, victimization, specialness, exclusion, etc.), you will see a neon sign saying EGO flash briefly.

    As you do, you will gently smile at it and say to yourself something to the effect of "Here goes my ego again. Isn't that funny?"
16. For all the situations above, remember to only observe and not judge (yourself or others).

◆

Here are a couple of examples where one might apply this exercise.

A wedding day is usually a joyous affair and might provide a good example of the type of honest assessment I am talking about. A lot of women look forward to and prepare for this day since being little

Ain't no sacrifice...at all

girls. But it's worth exploring the underlying reasons such as the need to be the center of attention, to have people admire her, congratulate her, telling her she's so pretty, etc. If the wedding is just the formalization of the love between 2 people, why make it a big hoopla with elaborate rituals around it? What is the couple's underlying reason for a big wedding as opposed to a small, simple, casual one? Is it the need to feel special (if only for a day)? Is it a (perhaps unconscious) desire to cause jealousy among single friends? Also think of the invited guests. Who was invited and who was excluded and why? What happens in the days following the wedding and honeymoon? For a lot of people, there is a sort of "now what?" letdown feeling afterwards. As we see, even with an event that is meant to be the symbol of love, there are usually a lot of egotistical undercurrents involved.

Another good example may be the birth of a child, which is traditionally meant to be a happy event. However, an honest assessment of why a couple decided to have a child could reveal some selfish and ego-driven reasons such as an arrogant pride of having created life, the need to feel special and be treated special by others (especially during pregnancy and after birth), the need to "pass on" one's genes or name (which reveals a misguided attachment to one's identity), the need to be admired and congratulated, the selfish desire to have someone there to love them, someone to care for them in their old age, etc. If you have children (or are considering having them), reflect on the above and have an honest assessment of your real motivations.

Perform a general self-assessment of your views of the world. Do you see a rosy picture? Do you only see the beauty and the good in the world, while ignoring (or being in denial of) its hideous side. What is your attitude when you watch the news? What are your feelings towards wars or other atrocities? Do you tend to feel sorry for one side and hatred for the other?

Again, these are just examples. I am not suggesting everyone feels any particular way, but just illustrating what the honest assessment process looks like. Note that you should perform this type of assessment with ordinary everyday life events as well (not just big life changing events).

By the way, if just reading these examples makes you upset, then this is a good sign that there is some underlying judgment involved. This is, of course, a great opportunity to practice forgiveness.

By working through these exercises, you will start to become more consciously aware of the true nature of the world, and thereby realize that you are not giving up anything at all by leaving it behind.

A GLIMPSE OF HOME

A Course in Miracles is not to be mastered intellectually, it is to be experienced. Learning every line of the text or being able to quote each workbook lesson may be an impressive feat, but by no means is it spiritual. It is only through the *experience* of the Course that one can hope to grow.

The idealists among us may be tempted to try to experience love, but true love cannot really be

Ain't no sacrifice...at all

experienced in this world as it is formless, eternal, changeless and total (which are heavenly attributes), whereas the world is based on form, time, change and separation. Only love's reflection (i.e. forgiveness) can be experienced here. Similarly, Oneness can only be experienced in heaven, but we can experience its reflection here as the joining (in mind) with others.

The Course incessantly reminds us of how joyful and indescribably blissful heaven is. But it is impossible to picture, let alone feel what that state might be like, since it is so unlike anything we experience here on earth. Workbook lesson 107 encourages us to imagine the most peaceful and blissful experience we ever encountered and multiply it 10,000 times and make it last forever. The lesson tells us that even this exercise would only give us a mere hint of what the state of heaven is like. Also this exercise is purely mental and still does not allow us to feel it in ourselves.

So, we are faced with a dilemma: we want to experience the state of heavenly joy, but are limited by the bounds of our body and brain.

This is where, I believe, hypnosis can be of tremendous help. By experiencing deep levels of hypnosis, we can get a sense of bliss that is not unlike the one described in the Course.

The Esdaile state (also known as "coma state") is a very deep state of hypnosis. It is named after Dr James Esdaile, an 18th century British surgeon who worked in India and performed many painless surgeries (including amputations) using hypnosis, without the use of any chemical anesthetics. Once in the Esdaile state, people are completely anesthetized. They cannot feel any pain, and the aesthesia can be just as powerful as with any chemical (and safer). The person is also fully paralyzed.

Hypnotic Spirituality

Their muscles are completely unresponsive. But they can still hear and understand any instruction given.

The state is usually described as one of total bliss. People also typically report profound emotional experiences of oneness and peace, with no pre-occupation for earthly issues, and no fear. The feeling is so blissful that those entering this state will usually be resistant to standard emerging instructions from the hypnotist, and stronger persuasion is required to get them out of that state (although they, of course, could never get "stuck" there; it's just that they are enjoying it so much that they are reluctant to leave).

This experience can be seen as a glimpse of leaving the body behind and becoming just a mind again. The feelings experienced match closely the state of blissfulness the Course describes, though certainly, in heaven, those feelings are infinitely stronger.

◆

So, in a way, the subconscious mind could be seen as a conduit that allows our heavenly (spiritual) self to seep through. And, the deeper we go into the subconscious mind, the closer we get to our real (Christ) Self and to our Source. Our conscious mind is more akin to the ego, in that it is concerned with worldly matters, and keeps us enslaved in our body and the world through its incessant monolog of regrets and guilt about the past and worries about the future. By bypassing it, we take one step towards the more peaceful, powerful us.

We also see that the deeper we go into a hypnotic state, the closer we get to a *bodiless*, pure mind, state of total bliss. This is a glimpse of what the Oneness with God must be like. I believe that, if deeper depths could be reached, they would continue to lead us back closer and closer to the state of Oneness (that we really never left).

Note that this exercise will not in itself heal your mind. But, it will provide you with an experience of what the state of heaven may be like. As a result, you will get a better sense for what the end goal is. If you were lacking the motivation to be diligent with your Course practice because you thought the "reward" was not worth that trouble, and heaven was not great enough to strive for, then this exercise should help you.

TIME WARP

In hypnosis, it is common for people to lose track of time. The deeper the trance, the faster time seems to pass. In deep levels such as the Esdaile state or Sichort state (see chapter 5 for details), this is even more pronounced. For instance, it's not uncommon for a client to emerge 20 minutes after the hypnotist asked them to do so and think the command was just given.

A Course in Miracles teaches us that time is an illusion, and that all the history of the universe (past, present and future) happened in an instant and is already over; we are actually all safe at home in the Oneness of God (and in fact, nothing ever happened at all).

As we go deeper into the state of hypnosis, time seems to move faster. And by extrapolating this reasoning, one could conclude that by going into deeper and deeper states of hypnosis, time would appear to speed to infinity, and would therefore cease to exist. For example, if under a medium level of hypnosis, 30 minutes of worldly time feels like, say, 10 minutes, and under a deep state of hypnosis they feel like a few seconds, then by extrapolation, one could conclude that, by reaching infinitely deep levels of trance, the billions of years of the universe would only feel like an instant. Phrased in a different way, our time on earth appears to be running a lot slower than it actually does. As the Course says, "The world was over long ago" (T-28.I.1:6); we are just reviewing its history *very very* slowly. So, once again, we can see how the state of hypnosis can help us experience a glimpse of our true (timeless) Self.

◆

We have seen that deep levels of hypnosis allow us to get a glimpse of our heavenly Self. In this state, we temporarily "lose" our body: we are filled with peace and bliss and time seems to run faster than it does out of hypnosis. This is, in my opinion, a very useful experience to motivate us in our Course practice as it gives us a sense of what we are striving for.

Experiencing deep states of trance such as the Esdaile or Sichort state is extremely beneficial. However, I do not recommend attempting to reach these states on your own using self-hypnosis. This should be conducted under the supervision of an experienced hypnotherapist.

We also discussed how triggers can be installed to make you aware of when you are in denial of the world's horrors. This will help you have a more honest view of the world.

The combination of these two exercises is, in my opinion, very valuable as you realize what little there is to give up in the world and what heaven promises.

Ain't no sacrifice...at all

These exercises make the choice for heaven an easy one. Use them to give yourself the motivation to be more assiduous in your Course practice or in the study of the techniques given in further chapters of this book.

As the "little willingness" section of the Text (T-18.I) says: "you find it difficult to accept the idea that you need give so little to receive so much."

CHAPTER TEN

-

BACK TO SCHOOL!

It is very tempting to spend our lives as if we were in jail. Indeed, this is the way most people live. They go about their day as if locked up in a giant prison called the world, from which there is no escape and where they are constantly tormented by other "inmates". Everybody is "out to get them", and every negative experience is just a reinforcement of their status of victim.

Another way to look at the world is as a school where you see every event that happens to you (good or bad) as an opportunity to learn a new lesson, and therefore as an opportunity to heal and release a "chunk" of repressed guilt. The world was created to keep us separated and reinforce our guilt. But, by seeing it as a school, we can turn the tables on the ego and use the world to learn forgiveness lessons and undo our guilt.

In this chapter, I will discuss the idea of viewing the world as a school and show you how you can apply it to your daily life. Hypnotherapy exercises will help you put these concepts into practice and accept them at an unconscious level of mind.

Back to school!

WELCOME TO YOUR NEW SCHOOL

In this school, the classroom is the world; the curriculum is your life and relationships; and ideally, the teacher is Jesus. I say "ideally" because we can learn from the ego or from Jesus (or Buddha or the Holy Spirit or whoever you want to think of as your guide). Choosing the right teacher is a central message of the Course. Moreover, you need to be humble enough to accept that you do not understand anything, otherwise you will not be open to learning. The too-cool-for-school attitude doesn't cut it, I'm afraid.

It is important to note that the learning occurs in the mind, not in the brain, the body or the world. As such, the learning continues even after the body has died. But, even though learning happens in the mind, Jesus has to teach you in the condition you think you are in (the body), and in the setting in which you think you are (the world).

It is also crucial to understand that since your life's tribulations constitute your curriculum, you should not deny the world or your experiences. Nor should you run away from civilization in the hope of staying away from negative experiences or relationships. Doing so would deprive your professor of the curriculum to teach from.

A CUSTOM CURRICULUM

As a starting point, consider each experience as a class that you can either pass or fail. If you fail, don't worry; you'll have many more opportunities to take it again (as many as necessary, over many lifetimes, and in

Hypnotic Spirituality

various forms). Make a conscious decision to start accepting the world and its adversity, instead of trying to fight it or fix it. Everything – and I mean absolutely everything – that happens in life is an opportunity to forgive something that is deeply buried within you, something that you did not know was there. So, do not deny what happens, but ask "what is the purpose of this (ego or Holy Spirit)?"

Like every good student, you need to pay attention in class. In particular, you need to pay attention to your body and its relationships. You have to see the problems as they are, not as you set them up (i.e. projecting them onto someone else). And you have to acknowledge *you* are the problem and are doing it to yourself. As a result, you will reverse the projection and see that the problem is inside you and not outside of you.

Another aspect of paying attention in class involves "rising above the battleground", and observing yourself and the situation. The world is inherently neither wonderful nor evil; it is neutral, it is nothing. And what makes something holy or unholy is not the form, nor what it looks like, nor any specific behavior, but the purpose that it serves. So, when facing a difficult situation or relationship, your response should be to observe it and ask "what can I learn from this? What is the purpose: love (Holy Spirit) or separation (ego)?" Again, don't deny the illusion, but change the way you look at things (your own life, wars, famines, the holocaust, football scores, political debates, etc.) from a victim/victimizer mentality to the notion that everybody is calling for the love they don't think they deserve.

◆

105

Back to school!

A good time to apply this new perception is when you're upset, angry, anxious, depressed, etc. First, acknowledge the fact that you feel that way. Don't pretend everything is OK. Don't pretend you are healed or holy, and always happy and peaceful. If you really felt that way, you probably would not be in this world, and you certainly would not need this book or the Course. It is better to accept the fact that you believe you are "unholy" and that you still have lessons to learn.

A Course in Miracles does not say that you should not get angry or upset or depressed or whatever; just that you should not justify these feelings by finding causes outside of you. Once you have acknowledged what you feel, ask to shift from the ego to the Holy Spirit, and ask "What would you have me do? What is the most loving thing to do?"

Now, when I say it's OK to feel upset, angry, etc., this is not an excuse to luxuriate in these feelings either. See the chapter "I've got the power" for more details on asking for help and making decisions.

A SELF-PACED COURSE

Try not to be too harsh on yourself regarding your progress. Jesus is a gentle teacher, and so should you be with yourself. It is unrealistic to expect perfection immediately.

The learning is progressive. On level 1, it's true that you are already healed. Therefore, in theory, you could instantly snap out of the dream. But, in practice, it does not work that way.

The fear of "going back" is so great that you need to adjust to it a little at a time. Just like your eyes need time

Hypnotic Spirituality

to adjust when going from a dark room into bright sunshine, you should expect your progress to be gradual. So, attempting perfection is not the goal.

For example, when doing the Workbook or studying the Text, it is better to be aware of what a "bad student" you are, and understand why (usually out of fear). If you don't do a lesson, but you realize and acknowledge that nobody or nothing is to blame for it but the fear of the lesson, then you have learned a great deal just by that recognition.

SOCIAL INTERACTION

Beside all the important things we learn in school (reading, writing, math, etc.), a vital part of going to school is our social interaction with other students. This has an important effect on how we develop into well-rounded, functioning adults. The same can be said about the school we're currently attending (the World). How you interact with other "students" is of paramount importance. Seeing others as separate and "out to get me" is detrimental to your spiritual progress. Instead, start seeing the face of Christ in others, overlooking their bodily appearance, and seeing them as nothing less than God-like. Achieving this will assist you in making tremendous progress.

Indeed, this recognition will allow you to start seeing the actions of others as either an expression of love or a call for love (which they think they are lacking), to which your response is love. Once again, it should be remembered that this occurs at the level of the mind, and the actual physical reaction in the world is irrelevant.

107

Here is a good exercise to practice this concept under hypnosis.

1. Imagine a friend.
2. See him in great detail, see his face, the way he moves, the sound of his voice.
3. Start seeing a faint light shining through his clothes emanating from his stomach. This is symbolizing the light of Christ that is within him.
4. See that light spreading throughout his body and intensifying, until all you see is a bright light and all his physical features have disappeared.
5. Repeat the exercise with several more people
6. Include people you dislike, find annoying or even hate.
7. Notice that the same light shines through them.
8. Imagine now a whole set of people going about their business and see them all turn into lights moving about like fire flies in a summer night.

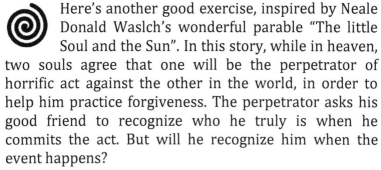 Here's another good exercise, inspired by Neale Donald Waslch's wonderful parable "The little Soul and the Sun". In this story, while in heaven, two souls agree that one will be the perpetrator of horrific act against the other in the world, in order to help him practice forgiveness. The perpetrator asks his good friend to recognize who he truly is when he commits the act. But will he recognize him when the event happens?

1. Induce a state of hypnosis
2. Remember a time when someone wronged you or really hurt you (physically or mentally).

Hypnotic Spirituality

3. See your reaction to the event and the feelings associated with it (anger, sadness, etc.)
4. Now see yourself and the other person floating back through time to the moment before this lifetime when you were plotting together the details of the event.
5. See how grateful you are to your friend for volunteering to give you such a wonderful forgiveness opportunity.
6. Now float back to the scene in this lifetime and replay it while seeing the other person for who He really is, remembering the agreement you made and feeling that same gratitude as you fully utilize this forgiveness opportunity.

WHEN DO I GRADUATE?

Now that you are increasingly able to view the world as a giant school and experience each event as a class, you may be wondering when you will be able to graduate. Here's a secret: you already have graduated! You could just go to the registrar's office right now, pick up your degree and frame it. But for some reason, you have not accepted that yet. So, you will keep coming back to class in this school, until you realize there is no class and no school in the first place.

How absurd is a school where the only thing you learn is that there is no need for school. Wait... that sounds a lot like my undergrad years...

Back to school!

IN PRACTICE

The school is an excellent metaphor for the world. If you can start seeing each experience, even the negative ones (especially the negative ones) and each relationship (especially the difficult ones) as a class and an opportunity to learn, this will lift a burden off your shoulders and contribute to your spiritual progress tremendously.

 You can apply this metaphor to your spiritual practice by visualizing yourself at school and transposing this feeling to real life situations. You can picture difficult circumstances as an opportunity to learn. Will you pass the test? If not, it's fine. Be gentle with yourself and acknowledge you are not ready for it yet. You will get as many chances to retake it as you need (perhaps in different forms).
1. Imagine a moment when you were upset
2. Ask to shift teacher from ego to Holy Spirit.
3. You now look forward to any interaction in the world, instead of dreading them, as you see them as a chance to learn a lesson and release some guilt.
4. Finally, picture other random students and see their body dissolve in your mind, to reveal the Christ in them.

Here's a sample session that applies these principles.

Chris' story

Chris had anger issues. In particular, he was prone to road rage. During the initial consultation, I discovered he was *A Course in Miracles* student. So, I decided his

Hypnotic Spirituality

session would include the school metaphor discussed above.

After establishing hypnosis, I started by asking Chris to visualize a school of his choice – be it one he attended or an imaginary one – and I asked him to describe it in detail, seeing himself as a student of this school, wearing a school uniform, taking classes, interacting with other students and faculty. I asked him to picture how eager he was to learn new material.

Next, I asked him to take this feeling with him and transfer it to a scene where he was driving on the highway, still wearing his school uniform, eager to learn from this class. I asked him to imagine, on the passenger seat, Jesus as his "driving instructor". As I described the traffic around him and people cutting him off, I could see Chris tense up a bit. I encouraged him to see this as a learning opportunity, to forgive himself and to acknowledge if he was not quite ready to pass this test yet.

Next, I suggested he decide to shift from an ego mindset to a Holy Spirit mindset. I also asked him to look in the other cars and picture the bodies of other drivers becoming more and more translucent, as a light in the center of their body became brighter and brighter. This image was designed to enable him to see his fellow students as Christ emanating love. His face gradually relaxed. I asked him to describe how he felt and he said he felt more comfortable, seeing the other drivers as neither good nor bad, and he did not perceive their erratic highway maneuvers as an attack. "I guess it's just the way they drive", he said.

We then went through a few more scenes which usually caused Chris to feel upset. Still wearing his school uniform, I asked him to approach each situation

Back to school!

with excitement and anticipation at the opportunity to learn a new lesson, and to see his fellow students for what they really were (Christ).

We concluded the session with a symbolic graduation ceremony where, as he came to the stage to receive his diploma, the dean and faculty disappeared, the students disappeared and the school slowly began to dissolve around him as I pointed out his diploma had been in his back pocket all along.

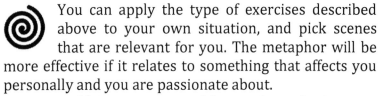

You can apply the type of exercises described above to your own situation, and pick scenes that are relevant for you. The metaphor will be more effective if it relates to something that affects you personally and you are passionate about.

Get yourself into a state of hypnosis and picture a situation that is upsetting to you. Then follow steps similar to Chris' example applying them to your situation.

Soon you will start seeing each of your interactions in the world as a class and an opportunity to learn.

CHAPTER ELEVEN

-

JUST AN ILLUSION

One of the key concepts of the Course that is crucial to its understanding (and unfortunately usually the hardest one to accept for most people) is that the world we see does not exist. In this chapter, we will review how the illusion came about, how we experience it and how we can use hypnosis to come to terms with the fact that a world that seems very real is in fact illusory.

HOW IT ALL STARTED

In order to understand the concept of illusion, we need to touch on the metaphysics of the Course. I will summarize here how the world came about (or seemed to). Please refer to Part 1 for a more detailed description of the mythology.

Our true nature is as Christ, "living" in a changeless, timeless, perfect Oneness with God. In that Oneness, an idea came to the Son that he could be separate from God. This is impossible, of course, but the Son took the idea seriously and believed the thought was capable of real

Just an Illusion

effects. The ego thought system was thus created. The ego convinced the Son that He had sinned, that God would punish Him for His sin, and that He needed a place to hide. Thus was the world made, and the Son of God started separating into billions of fragments (not just humans but also animals, vegetables, minerals and everything in the universe). As soon as the error was made, it was instantly corrected (Holy Spirit thought system), and we were left with a split mind and a Decision Maker that can choose between the two sides. The ego set up a sophisticated system to keep us rooted in the world to make it appear so real that we forget our initial mistaken choice (or that we even have a choice).

PROJECTION

One major mistake we need to reverse is the idea that the world is doing things *to* us. The Course says "ideas leave not their source" (W.pI.156.1:3; W.pI.167.3:6,7), which means that the world we see is really a projection of our thoughts. As a matter of fact, the only value the world has is that it shows us what's in our mind. You can think of it as a mirror of the mind.

The perceived sin in us is so enormous that we cannot handle it; we deny it and project it onto other characters, so that we can point an accusing finger at the "sinner" who attacked us unjustifiably.

By realizing that the experiences in the world are not done *to* you but *by* you, you can start reversing the projection and take responsibility. This is what the Buddha meant when he said "I am awake". He realized he was a cause and not an effect.

Hypnotic Spirituality

The use of imagery and metaphors in hypnosis can help us work towards this realization. Here is an example I've used, but feel free to come up with your own.

1. Induce a state of hypnosis
2. Imagine yourself in a movie theater watching a movie.
3. But the movie you are watching is peculiar in the sense that it is a movie of your life.
4. See yourself as the main protagonist and watch common events of your life unfold on the screen.
5. You can make it more realistic by making it a 3D movie if you wish.
6. Disassociate from the "you" sitting in the theater and float up to the projection booth hidden at the very back of the theater.
7. From here, imagine the movie originating from your head and projecting onto the huge screen.
8. Whatever you think gets projected onto the screen. Any bad thought about yourself, anything you may feel guilty about gets projected outside of yourself and onto a character, situation or event on the screen.
9. Now, transport yourself from the movie theater to a normal everyday scene in your life such as work, at home with your family, or simply walking in the street.
10. Become aware of how the all characters of that scene are originating from the projector in your head.
11. Experience how you are the ultimate creator of your reality – whether you feel good or bad, happy,

115

lonely, angry, anxious, joyful, victimized or anything else. It is you who is creating that experience.
12. Realize that you can choose again, that you are the cause and not the effect.

We need to be careful with this metaphor since there will be a temptation to think the projection comes from your brain and that you are real but those "other" people are not. It's important to remember your body and brain are just as illusory as anybody else's and the projection is really in the mind outside of time and space.

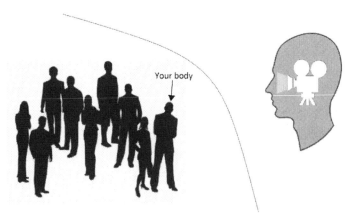

THE TIME OF MY LIFE

Even harder to accept than the illusion of the physical world is the illusion of time. When the separation seemed to occur, the whole world of time and space was created in an instant. And, in one instant, it was immediately corrected by the Holy Spirit.

The entire script of the universe was thus written in that one moment, and this script can be used to serve the ego's purpose or the Holy Spirit's. When we see time and space and the events happening in our life, we are, in effect, reviewing this script. How we review it and with whom (the ego or the Holy Spirit) is the only question.

In fact, we each possess the entire history of the universe in our mind, and at any point, we can decide to re-experience any part of it. It is therefore more accurate to think of time as holographic rather than linear.

◆

A hologram can be created by splitting a laser beam in two (using a half mirror), illuminating an object with one beam (called the object beam), and recording on a medium the interferences of this beam with the other beam (called the reference beam).

The following figure illustrates this process in a very simplified way.

Just an Illusion

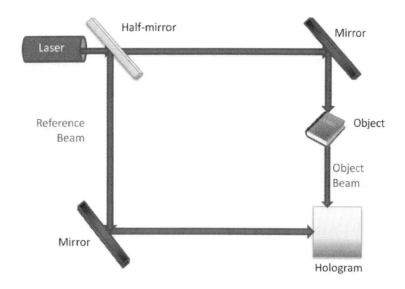

The resulting hologram recorded on the medium appears to be a random pattern. But, when you illuminate it with the same laser used originally (reference beam), it recreates the image of the original object.

Interestingly, if you cut the hologram in half, you do not end up with two halves of the object as you would with a photograph. Instead, each half contains the whole picture – albeit a bit fainter. The process can be repeated many times, and each bit of hologram still retains the entire image.

This, in my opinion, is a very good metaphor for the way we could view the illusion. The writing of the script is akin to the creation of the hologram. And, even though the Son shattered into billions of fragments, each one of these fragments retains the entire story within itself. We can refine this analogy by imagining that two separate laser beams were used and shined at the script (one laser representing the ego, the other the Holy Spirit) and recorded as holograms in an instant. Now, when we want to "recreate" a particular scene of this holographic script, we can decide to use either the ego's laser beam or the Holy Spirit's. Therefore, we can choose to perceive any part of the script in two different ways.

This metaphor can be recreated under hypnosis.

1. Take yourself into a state of trance.
2. Picture the moment of the (seeming) separation
3. Imagine the huge script of the history of the world being written in a flash. You can visualize the script as a big book or perhaps a long scroll.
4. Picture the two beams (ego and Holy Spirit) each creating a hologram of the script.
5. Now, fast forward to today
6. Picture these holograms on a table and see yourself holding the two laser devices, one in each hand, ready to illuminate their hologram.
7. Which beam will you use?
8. Which view of the script (and therefore the world) will you choose?

◆

Just an Illusion

A seeming paradox of the Course is that, even though it teaches time is an illusion, it says that following the Course can save us many years. Though it does not directly talk about re-incarnation, the Course implies that our healing is spread over many lifetimes. By applying the Course's principle of forgiveness, you learn lessons, and in the process, release a chunk of guilt. Without the practice of forgiveness, it would take a long time to learn each lesson. So, in this way, you do not have to experience as many forms of each individual lesson and therefore you save time. It's a bit like skipping chapters on a DVD.

The concept of time can also be seen as a representation of the original sin/guilt/fear: I have sinned in the past, therefore I feel guilty now and I am fearful that God will punish me in the future. In a way, every issue we encounter in the world is a re-enactment of our initial (seeming) separation and the resulting sin, guilt and fear.

Eventually, when you accept the Atonement for yourself, time (indeed the entire universe) will disappear. Therefore, paradoxically, time's only purpose is to teach us that time does not exist. It keeps us rooted in the world, until we have learned enough lessons that it ceases to exist. So, we can see time as just a teaching device that will only be there until the point where it is no longer required.

1. In hypnosis, picture yourself standing on a bright line (perhaps like a giant neon light) stretching from infinity behind you to infinity in front of you.
2. Float up from the line

Hypnotic Spirituality

3. Picture yourself in your wrong mind, and see yourself move along the line at a snail's pace.
4. Then, imagine yourself in your right mind, practicing forgiveness, and see yourself zip along the line at a very fast speed.
5. Repeat this a few times, switching between right and wrong mind
6. Notice the speed at which you move in both cases.
7. Also realize that, as you move forward, the line is becoming fainter and fainter.
8. Continue the exercise until you have moved so far forward on the line that it becomes so faint it eventually disappears.

◆

We have already discussed that, in an instant, the script was written and corrected. It all already happened, and our "life" consists of choosing which part of the script to re-experience and, more importantly, which teacher we will experience it with. Each episode is an opportunity to learn a lesson. The ultimate lesson is that the Son is sinless (which is reflected in seeing our shared interest and shared nature as Christ). We have actually already accepted this lesson (and all lessons for that matter). *When* we choose to re-experience it is the only decision. We've all accepted the Atonement, even though, in the illusion of time, it seems that we're a long way from achieving it. The sole question is how long we decide to stay asleep in our misery. Every time we choose not to align with the Holy Spirit's view, we are only adding to the agony. It is not sinful, but it is silly to make this last longer than we need to. So, we should be grateful for any opportunity that is presented to us to

Just an Illusion

learn a lesson, as it is a chance for us to move towards our ultimate goal – which is also the starting point we never left...

 Here's a helpful analogy that has been used for this concept:

1. Imagine a DVD player and two stacks of seemingly identical DVDs.
2. However, each movie was filmed twice and stored on a separate disk (one labeled "Ego" and one "Holy Spirit").
3. Visualize two stacks of DVDs,
4. For each movie, see yourself making choices from one of the stacks.
5. Picture yourself watching a particular movie, but for each scene swapping disks and watching either the ego version or the Holy Spirit version.
6. Get in touch with the negative feelings resulting from watching the ego version and the positive feelings from watching the Holy Spirit version.

This is a helpful metaphor, but it still has the implication of linearity, in that you can only watch one DVD at a time and when you're done, you move to another one. In reality, all events happened simultaneously.

 I prefer a slight variation on this theme, where movies are stored in computer files.

1. Imagine two versions of each file, one with a *.ego* extension and one with a *.hs* extension (e.g.: wife_nagging.ego and wife_nagging.hs)

122

2. You can launch the movies by double-clicking on one version of the file or the other.
3. Open as many files (each representing a different lesson) as you want, and have them tiled in little windows on the screen. This represents that all lessons are learned simultaneously since time is illusory.
4. As you learn a lesson, the corresponding window closes, the file disappears, along with all files with the same content (but in different form).
5. Continue this process until all files have disappeared from the computer, at which point the computer itself evaporates... and so do you.

THE ULTIMATE REPRESSED THOUGHT

Traumas experienced as a child are often repressed and hidden from the conscious mind, because they were too difficult to handle at the time. Instead of facing them, memories are buried in the subconscious mind, along with the emotions attached to them.

By hiding these thoughts from conscious awareness, we fool ourselves into believing the event did not happen. However, their effects are still felt, since the subconscious remains aware of them and creates often undesirable symptoms in reaction to them.

The subconscious works in mysterious ways, and its associations are not always logical. The traumatic event that has been repressed is often called the Initial Sensitizing Event (I.S.E.). Please refer to the "Methods of Hypnotherapy" chapter in Part 2 for more details on this subject and examples.

Just an Illusion

According to *A Course in Miracles*, guilt over the seeming separation from God is the cause of the world and the body. But we are so rooted in the illusion that we are not even aware of our decision to want to separate from God. This means our guilt of separation is the ultimate repressed thought and the (seeming) separation the ultimate ISE.

The repression of past traumas is one of the main causes of psychosomatic symptoms in people. This is especially true when the traumas were experienced as a child. One common technique used in hypnotherapy is to "regress" the person back to the ISE. It is not possible to change the actual event that caused the trauma, but it is possible to change the way the individual perceives it and feels about it. This, in turn, changes the effect the repressed thought had on the individual. The client revivifies (similar to reliving) the traumatic event, which is usually accompanied by an abreaction (an emotional and often tearful reaction). After reviewing the memory a number of times, the emotion subsides, and the client begins to see the event in a different light, with his now-adult understanding. This process has the effect of releasing the hold that the event and its associated emotions have over the person, and if fully released, leads to symptom removal and long-term healing.

It does not matter how insignificant the ISE appears to us now; if it was perceived as tragic or traumatic by the child, it can often have severe effects on the individual later in life. The severity of the symptoms is also unpredictable and can range from a slight tic, to an "allergy" to a particular food, to full-blown panic attacks, for example. Whatever the symptoms, healing can be achieved by revisiting the originating cause of the issue and releasing bottled up emotions during the

Hypnotic Spirituality

revivification process. As long as this process is fully complete, total symptom removal should be achieved.

◆

The parallels to the Course are clear. Miracle principle number one teaches us that there's no order of difficulty in miracles. In other words, according to the Course, all problems are illusory, so no matter how minor or severe they appear to be, all issues are the same.

We can theorize that applying hypnotherapy techniques and going back to the ultimate ISE (i.e. our perceived separation from God) would lead to our salvation. Now, I am not suggesting that a hypnotherapy session could lead to our salvation. I wish it were that easy. This ultimate ISE is too deeply buried, beyond even the subconscious. Also, the potential abreaction (facing our guilt) would most likely be extremely emotional. As a matter of fact, it is way too frightening for most of us to even contemplate at this point in our spiritual development.

 However, we can make strides towards it by visualizing this ISE and the world that unfolded from it.

1. Induce a state of hypnosis
2. Imagine the moment of the separation using any symbol or character that you are comfortable with.
3. Picture the chain of events that followed from that decision (see also the timeline exercise later in this book).
4. See the creation of the universe, various events in history and finally culminating with your birth

125

Just an Illusion

This is still illusory, but I believe bringing this event into awareness can help us accept the unreality of the world. And, this is a great first step towards our real salvation.

PEOPLE SAY I'M A DREAMER...
AND I *AM* THE ONLY ONE

Indeed, you can think of the world as a dream. You are the dreamer, and all the characters in the dream are made up. You are responsible for everything that happens in the dream.

In Jungian dream analysis theory, the characters of the dream are self-created and represent an unacknowledged aspect of the dreamer. Even though they are part of the psyche of the dreamer, they are perceived as external entities in the dream. They usually are represented as symbols in the dream, since the true nature of the associated thought is too horrible for the dreamer to face directly. Those dream characters provide a metaphor that still conveys the same message but in a form that is more palatable.

Similarly, when the thought of separation was projected outside of the mind, the world and the body arose. All characters in the dream are projections of our thoughts, even though we perceive them as external. Here also, the characters of the dreams are metaphors for the terrible inner guilt projected out in symbolic form. Just like a dream, the scene feels real and we are convinced that what is happening is real when it is really only in the mind.

Workbook lesson 23 teaches that "you see the image you made but don't see yourself as the image maker". In other words, you see the world you're dreaming, but

126

don't see yourself as the dreamer. And, therein lies the problem. The issue is not what goes on in the dream; the issue is that you *are* dreaming at all, and you don't realize you are. So, there is no way you can effect change, because what needs to be changed is the decision in your mind. Trying to manipulate the dream, make it make sense and make it "work" for you is bound to fail. Instead, you should change the cause of the dream (the decision in your mind to have chosen the ego).

◆

The Course tells us that there are actually two levels of the dream: the world's dream (our life) and the "secret dream" (the guilt and seeming evil in our mind). One takes place in the body and the world and the other in the mind. But, their cause is the same: the dreamer, and the fact that you have forgotten that you are the dreamer. So, you may want to remind yourself that you are the cause of everything you feel. You are the dreamer of your dream of victimization, vengeance, hate, despair, depression, death, betrayal, etc. Bring to your awareness the fact that, at any moment, you can choose to feel differently. And if you don't, it's because you don't want to. Nobody is responsible but you. It is a sobering but liberating thought.

Freud also argues that dreams represent the fulfillment of a wish. In the section *Self Concept vs. Self,* the Course says "If you can be hurt by anything, you see a picture of your secret wish [to hurt]. Nothing more than this. And in your suffering of any kind, you see your own concealed desire to kill" (T-31.V.15:8-10). Your "desire to kill" may not be a literal one (i.e. an inclination to commit murder). What this section refers to is your putting on the "face of innocence" and pointing an accusing finger at the alleged victimizers or wrong-doers hoping God will punish them instead of you. So, it's a desire to kill by God-proxy in a way. Bringing this secret desire into your awareness and coming to grips with it is of tremendous help in your spiritual quest.

 A good exercise is to leverage the lucid dreamer analogy. A lucid dreamer is one who is in a dream, but is aware that he is dreaming, and can exert control on the dream.
1. Induce a state of hypnosis.
2. Picture yourself falling asleep and starting to dream.
3. Step into the dream and see scenes of everyday life or fantasy scenes.
4. Be fully aware this is a dream.
5. Imagine you are wearing a bracelet that says "Dream".
6. Picture the scenes in vivid details and interact with others in the dream.
7. Occasionally glance at your wrist and see the bracelet reminding you that you are only dreaming.
8. Feel the peace coming from that realization.

This will help you subconsciously accept the idea that your life is really a dream.

◆

So why doesn't Jesus just shake us up to awaken us? Imagine, you are sitting by your son's bed and you see he's having a nightmare. You would not just shake him up and yell at him to wake up. It would be too frightening. You would gently talk to him, knowing he can hear your voice and maybe stroke his arm to calm him down. That's a good way to think about Jesus: a soothing voice coming from outside the dream gently reminding us that this is just a dream and that we can wake up when we're ready and everything will be all right.

THE BEST SCREEN EVER

Screen memories are a common occurrence in therapy, be it psychotherapy or hypnotherapy. A screen memory is part of the subconscious resistance mechanism; it is a memory of an event that comfortably explains why the client has his symptoms. In other words, it attempts to mask the real problem from consciousness, and the purpose of the substitution is to "screen" (i.e. protect oneself from) painful conflict-laden recollections.

The notion of "screen memories" was first presented by Freud in his paper of the same name. Later, he determined that these memories supplied the best available source of knowledge about the "forgotten" childhood years (if interpreted correctly, of course). Any memory could be a screen memory when one aspect of it screens out something unacceptable to the ego.

A screen memory (like forgetting and amnesia) is a compromise between repressed elements and the defense against them. As screen memories cover up that which is unacceptable to the ego, they may be considered essentially defensive in nature.

If the screen memories are sufficiently traumatic and/or bizarre, victims may spend so much time fixating on them and trying to understand them, that they never

Just an Illusion

get past them (and get to what the screen memories were designed to block out).

A good example is given by Freud in one of his papers. He recounts one of his own memories of childhood (though he attributed it to someone else), in which he saw himself playing with other kids in a green field scattered with yellow flowers. Through analysis, a later (teenage) memory surfaced, one of a girl he loved wearing a yellow dress. Therefore, the childhood memory was just a screen for a later sexual desire and Freud concluded that "there was *no* childhood memory, but only a fantasy put back into childhood".

Another example is found in Freud's *Psychopathology of Everyday Life*. A man recalls a memory of himself as a 5-year-old child, sitting with his aunt and asking her how to tell the difference between an 'm' and an 'n'. The aunt points out that the m had an extra portion (stroke) to it. The memory sounds innocent, but it was found later that this was masking his curiosity about the difference between boys and girls (an extra portion), and he would have wanted that this aunt be his *teacher*.

◆

In the context of the Course's teachings, the world and the body are the ultimate screen memory designed by the ego to keep us mindless and prevent us from ever looking inside. It is set up to hide the tremendous guilt we felt over the (seeming) separation and our fear that God was about to destroy us.

Note that it is indeed just a memory of sorts, since the script has already happened and we're just reviewing it mentally. Who we review it with (ego or Holy Spirit) is what matters.

Hypnotic Spirituality

The Course aims to help us realize this is a screen memory and look past it. In the same way they can bring to light screen memories, the hypnotherapy techniques discussed in this book can help us recognize the true nature of the illusion and see the world for what it really is.

HIERARCHY OF ILLUSIONS

Another key concept of the Course's view of the illusion is that there is no hierarchy of illusions. Or stated differently, as in miracle principle number one, there is no order of difficulty in miracles. Since the world is wholly unreal, there isn't one part that is more or less real than any other. Only our perception creates such differences. In other words, we create arbitrary groups of people and objects, and arrange them in hierarchies of preferences and judgments. For instance, we'll assign values to objects in a form such as "this pen is less valuable than this sofa which is less valuable than my house". Or "a stranger's body is less valuable than my spouse's body, which is less valuable than my own body". Every object or body is actually neutral (since they are all equally illusory) but we instinctively assign values to them. The Course helps us realize that there is indeed no value in anything in the illusion.

The ego always sees the world as one or the other. If one is up, the other down; if one is guilty, the other is innocent; if one is right, the other is wrong, etc. The ego does not know the meaning of "same". Its existence is predicated on the idea that God and the Son are separate and different; and therefore, everything is different.

So, the world appears inherently made of different parts of various shapes, sizes, colors, etc. And we see

Just an Illusion

things (as well as our thoughts) only in contrast with each other.

Similarly, some problems seem harder to solve than others. Beating Lebron James in a one-on-one game of basketball seems more difficult than beating, say, your little nephew. Some diseases (such as AIDS or cancer) seem harder to heal than others (such as a mild headache). And, some things upset us more than others (Hitler's atrocities vs. your spouse's nagging about taking the garbage out). The only reason these differences seem real is that we *want* them to be. We are so attached to our identity and the ego that, if we were to accept the truth, it would mean the ego does not exist and, as a result, we do not exist either. This is a terrifying prospect for most people. We do not want to lose our identity and give up the ego's dream, so we convince ourselves that things are real and their hierarchies are meaningful.

By a process of selective perception, we seek to find in the world proofs of the judgments we made in our mind. For instance, a racist may have decided that all people of a certain color are lazy, and as he goes about his daily life, will subconsciously look for and retain evidence that reinforces this belief, while ignoring all evidence to the contrary. This is a process similar to what we described in the section on the Conscious Critical Faculty (see Part 2).

Remember that it's only our *choice* for illusions that makes them real. In other words, just like the racist who looks for evidence to justify his prejudice, we have decided some illusions are better than others, and only see evidence that prove it, while discarding evidence to the contrary.

132

Hypnotic Spirituality

Another form of hierarchy and judgment relates to our customs. Some people consider themselves more holy or spiritual than others based on the clothes they wear (or refuse to wear), the food they eat (or refuse to eat) and the things they do (or refuse to do). As the Course repeatedly states, whatever we wear, eat or do in the world does not matter; what matters is the purpose behind them. The issue comes from the fact that these customs have the goal of dividing instead of uniting, as they differentiate one group from another. The following of customs by a particular group is often accompanied by a smug arrogance and an air of superiority, implying that others who do not follow these practices are less worthy than those who do.

Moreover, by placing value on one thing (be it an article of clothing or a type of food) over another, they reaffirm their belief that there *is* a hierarchy of illusions, and that some illusions are better than others, which of course, only reinforces the error.

Let's use food as an example. The body was created to always be in a state of need and lack (in total opposition to heaven, where we lack nothing). It always needs to take the next breath, eat more, drink more, etc. in order to survive. And it does so at the expense of someone or something else (a key ego concept). For instance, with every breath we take, we ingest (and therefore destroy) thousands of micro-organisms. And, every time we eat, we kill and cannibalize another creature or plant (as much a part of the Sonship as we are). Such is the way of the body. But, by placing more value on one type of food over another, one reinforces the belief in hierarchies. A piece of chicken or fish is just as illusory as a turnip or a carrot. So, by assigning more value to one than the other, and by considering (not) eating a particular food a

133

spiritual practice, they are, in effect, falling into the trap of the ego's thought system and its hierarchy of illusions, thereby moving in the wrong direction spiritually, or at the very least limiting their progress.

◆

As we grow spiritually, we start to be more willing to let go of our identity (individual or group). As we do, we stop clinging to those arbitrary groupings and judgments; and as a result, the hierarchy flattens out, so to speak. We stop seeing evidence of differences, and we stop seeing things having more value than others.

We can then start to slowly generalize that process, until it includes everything, and we fully realize that all things are equal in their illusory nature.

Here's a simple exercise you can do under hypnosis to get this process started:

1. Imagine two problems: one that you can easily handle and another that is giving you trouble and is really upsetting you.
2. Picture a screen with the first problem projected on it.
3. See it in detail and place that image in the top right corner of the screen.
4. Picture the second problem.
5. See it in detail and place the image in the bottom left corner of the screen.
6. Look at the top right corner image and feel how easy it is to handle it.
7. Drag it to the bottom left image, bringing along the feelings of ease from the top right.

Hypnotic Spirituality

8. As the two images merge together, see them starting to fade and slowly disappear, thereby symbolizing the unreality of both.
9. You can repeat this exercise with a few different topics.

After a while, these will become unconscious, and you will start generalizing this principle to other situations.

BODY OF EVIDENCE

Our most prized possession and the best "evidence" that the world is real is our body. However, as we saw in the preceding section, there is no hierarchy of illusion. Therefore, our body is no more real or valuable than any other objects in the world.

Worshiping the body and cultivating it in an attempt to get happiness is therefore a futile and misguided exercise. Just like anything else outside of us, it cannot truly make us happy or unhappy. Some swing the pendulum the other way, arguing that, since the body is unreal and valueless, there's no point in maintaining it. So, they follow unhealthy practices and let their body and mind deteriorate to the point where they can't function properly in the world (and therefore cannot learn the lessons offered to them). This is obviously not the right attitude either.

As usual, the solution is not in what you actually do or don't do, but in the purpose behind it. If working with the Holy Spirit as your teacher, your actions will represent the most loving thing to do; and that may be taking care of your body. This is OK as long as you realize it is unreal and will not, in and of itself, lead to

Just an Illusion

your salvation. You need to remember that the world is a classroom, in which we come to learn lessons. If you do not take care of your body and die an early death, you may miss out on valuable opportunities to learn lessons. It is, in a way, a form a suicide. There's nothing inherently sinful about suicide; it's just a decision to not learn lessons in this lifetime and delay the learning to a future lifetime. But, why wait?

The body itself can be an excellent source of lessons when it is stricken by disease. Here again, you have two choices: you can either see the disease as an unfair attack on you from a cruel world. This will only reinforce your victim mentality, and therefore your guilt, keeping you rooted in the world. Or, you can see the disease for what it is: a projection of your guilt, and therefore an opportunity to acknowledge that guilt without judgment, and retain your peace. In that sense, the body can serve a positive purpose.

So, we need to accept that it's not the body that is sick but the mind (separation and guilt). In the end, the purpose of the body and world is to realize there is no body or world.

◆

We have covered a lot of ground in this chapter. We have discussed the illusion of time and space and how this world can be seen as a dream or likened to a repressed screen memory. We have worked through several exercises to come to grips with the illusory nature of our world and the fact that it is a projection from our mind. Finally, we've discussed hierarchies of illusions and how our perception of them affects us.

In the next chapter, we discuss another important concept: victimization.

CHAPTER TWELVE

-

FACE LIFT

An important aspect of the ego thought system that *A Course in Miracles* exposes is our habit of portraying ourselves as innocent victims. Because of the tremendous guilt we experienced over the seeming separation from God (and the fear of God's vengeance), we are always on the lookout for others to blame.

We put on the *face of innocence*, and point accusingly at our parents, spouse, colleagues, world leaders, etc. to demonstrate how unfairly treated we are, and how guilty everybody else is.

We create a world and project our guilt onto others, so we can say "look I'm an innocent victim; those other people are clearly the sinners and *they*, not I, deserve God's punishment".

In this chapter, we will examine how we display this "face of innocence", and how we can reverse that trend and take responsibility for our world.

THE BLAME GAME

One of the great tools in the ego's arsenal of tricks to keep us rooted in the world is (perceived) victimization. Everywhere we turn, we seem to be confronted with evidence that we are unfairly treated. This stems from the initial mistake of the (seeming) separation. Once we thought we separated, we were overwhelmed with guilt as we believed we had *killed* God. This was quickly followed by fear that God would take vengeance, so we created a world in which to "hide". We started fragmenting into billions of pieces, which we could then project our guilt onto. Fearing God's retribution, we set up situations where we are victimized in some form. This way, we (think we) get rid of our sin; it's no longer in us, it's in someone else (be they parents, siblings, colleagues, bosses, political leaders, etc.). Surely, God will punish them – not poor innocent me – for their sins.

As we will discuss in Chapter 15 ("I've got the power"), if you set the goal to be a victim, you go around looking for people to victimize you or reject you, and will experience what you wished.

We relish every opportunity to see the sin and guilt in others. This is why people love violence on TV or in movies, and horrific stories in the news: because they see the sin and it's not in them; it's in those horrible people "out there".

It can sometimes be very subtle and innocent. For instance, have you ever noticed, at the office, when the power or network goes down and people temporarily can't work, instead of the frustration of having their work interrupted, there's a subtle sense of euphoria, as people relish the fact that they can't work because of someone else (the power company, the network engineers, etc.).

It's important to note that this is not a trait we develop as we grow. Babies are born with fully grown egos, and the mere fact that they are in the world proves it. They are, in fact, the epitome of the face of innocence: demanding to be fed, rocked, washed, changed, etc., and screaming the place down if their needs are not met. "Look at me, I am powerless and at the mercy of a cruel world", they seem to say. What a perfect cover! As we grow older, we are taught to "behave" and social conditioning forces us to hide this demanding, selfish ego under a façade of courtesy and politeness. The ego remains intact nevertheless; we just get better at disguising it.

◆

Since the victimizers are projections from our mind, when we portray ourselves as innocent victims (emotionally or physically), we are really revealing our secret dream to hurt and victimize. Under the face of innocence is really the face of guilt, attack and murder. So, in a way, we are victims only of our thoughts. Since we're not aware of the projection, the attacks of others seem unjustified, which allows us to claim we were unfairly treated. Some even build a whole identity on what was done to them, and relish every opportunity to tell everyone about it.

Note that we've been talking about the victimizer as if it were an individual, but it can just as well be a thing such as a microbe, a virus or any element that causes a disease; it can be a group such as the city council who passed an ordinance unfavorable to you, the company

Face Lift

which laid you off or a country which seems threatening; it can even be a more abstract entity like the stock market, the weather or "society".

I also want to point out that, as with everything the Course prescribes, this happens at the level of the mind and not the level of form. Your behavior in the world may remain the same, and you may continue to act "normally", but your perception at the level of mind will be different.

TAKING RESPONSIBILITY

As you know, the real power is in the mind. By being mindless (the ego's goal for us all), you are powerless, and therefore a victim. In order to get out of this mad scheme, you need to first realize you *have* a mind and the power to choose. All feelings of victimization should be seen as a choice you made. You *wanted* that headache, that abuse, that rain that ruined your golf outing, that greedy CEO who embezzled money and made your stock go down, etc. You chose them so you could blame someone or something outside of you for it. But, since you now know there's nothing outside, you have to accept responsibility for it. By blaming others, you are really accusing yourself. So, it's not the virus, your spouse's shrieking or the food you ate that made you sick, since there is nothing outside. How can you blame *nothing*?

You need to acknowledge that there is a causal connection between how you feel (not great) and the goal you set (you made decisions with the ego, instead of the Holy Spirit). The ego will argue that you feel this way because, for example, your boss is mean, your children

142

Hypnotic Spirituality

are sick, or your business is not doing well. But, the real reason you feel this way is because you chose the ego and turned away from the Holy Spirit.

You make yourself sick, for example, because it provides you with a convenient cover to not experience the peace of God. Since you forget you set the goal, you don't realize that what happens to you is your choice. All you see is the shadow or the mirror of what's within you, and by realizing this, you become aware that there *is* an inside; therefore there *is* a mind; therefore, there *is* a choice. And therein lies the hope.

If you are upset, it's because you chose to be, but instead of accepting responsibility, you project it onto someone else and say that the reason you're not happy is because of XYZ... You can think of the anger you feel towards the victimization as a defense against the fear of accepting responsibility for your own guilt.

So, start seeing the investment you have in perceiving yourself unfairly treated, and realize that this investment only serves the ego. The awareness of this victimization attitude is the first step. When accusing someone of something, the Course suggests you ask yourself: "Would I accuse myself of that?"

As with everything that happens in the world, we can see it through the eyes of the ego or the Holy Spirit. To take an extreme example, if you are in a concentration camp in Auschwitz, the ego's interpretation would clearly be one of victim. But, you could instead remain at peace and see it as a way to learn that the Nazis are as much a part of the Sonship as you, and their actions are really a call for love.

As you learn to not see yourself as a victim, you heal the associated guilt, and save time on your trip back home. If there's no guilt, there's no fear related to that

143

Face Lift

guilt, so there's no need to deny it, and therefore no need to project it (remember that the guiltless mind is healed).

This is, of course, easier said than done, and it is not realistic to expect to forgo this victim mentality 100% of the time. When you don't, it is better to acknowledge it, tell yourself you know what you're doing (i.e. you want to blame someone/something else in order to be special) and that's ok. Don't fight yourself, forgive yourself instead. Forgive yourself because, as stated in the Course, your heart is filled with *darkness and murder.* Remember that "forgiveness...is still, and quietly does nothing.... It merely looks, and waits, and judges not." (W-pII.1.4:1,3)

IN PRACTICE

Hypnotherapists around the world would confirm that many of their clients perceive themselves as victims. Our culture seems to increasingly become one of entitlement and prone to blame someone or something (be it the government, corporations, the media, "society", etc.) for its woes. So, even outside the context of the Course or any spiritual practice, many people have benefited greatly from realizing that they do have control over their thoughts. Once helped to realize that it's their *perception* of a given situation, not the situation itself that is causing their issues, they generally see the error of their ways and feel a lot better about themselves.

Hypnotherapists spend time helping their clients become aware that they are not responsible for the horrific things that happened to them; for example, to see the abuse they suffered as a child as "not their fault". Therapy is geared towards helping them let go of past traumas, so that they see them in a different light consciously. Meanwhile, the unconscious also has the opportunity to reclassify and "refile" particular memories so that they are not referenced in the same way in the future. The aim is that there will be a neutral (rather than negative) response to these memories following therapy.

I diverge from these conventional therapies when working with Course students. Healing the past is an extraordinarily beneficial experience for everyone. However, with Course students, it is possible to go one step further, enabling them to realize at a deeper level of mind that they are the author of their script, and that all perceived attacks of which they are "victims" are really projections of their own guilt.

I generally follow these steps:

1. Working on shedding that "face of innocence" so that they realize their mind is the source of the attacks and victimization.
2. Install triggers to raise conscious awareness of future situations where they feel unfairly treated. This reminds them of their error and to let go of any guilt related to their negative reaction.
3. We then work on forgiveness which takes this process one step further and teaches them to forgive others - and therefore themselves - for what they have not done. Forgiving people for what they have not done can be interpreted at the metaphysical level (it's all an illusion so nothing really happened) but, in practice, it's easier for most

Face Lift

people to think of it as "what they have not done is take the peace away from me".

4. So, the last logical step is to practice keeping your inner peace no matter what is done "to" you (more on that in upcoming chapters).

The process is, of necessity, progressive. Initially, it is not realistic to expect to withhold judgment against everyone and in every situation. Maybe, at the beginning, you can focus on small things such as someone who stepped on your foot or did not give you the correct change at the counter. Then, you can go on to generalize that principle progressively to all people and situations.

Jamie's story

Jamie was a 33-year old restaurant manager, and was the poster child of perceived victimization. He initially consulted for depression, and it quickly became clear that he had a knack for seeing every situation as an unfair treatment and every person as a victimizer of sorts.

He was kind-hearted and spiritual, so we discussed some of the Course aspects (especially the ones described in this chapter), and he seemed to understand and accept the concepts, at least on an intellectual level. But, I could tell that he had not absorbed them fully (but, in fairness, who among us really has...), and had not fully realized how they applied to him.

Over the course of his hypnotherapy sessions, we worked through some exercises similar to the one described above and in previous chapters. We went through a projection simulation, so that he could feel everyday situations coming from him. We also played several scenes of "victimization", either imaginary or from his life, and used NLP techniques under hypnosis to change the perception of the scene. Finally, we went deeper in the application of Course principles, and worked through some exercises where he saw the "unfair treatment" as a decision *he* made.

After these sessions, his view of the world started to change, as he slowly stopped seeing every situation as an attack and everyone as a victimizer. As he started to perceive situations differently and taking more responsibility for his life, his depressed mood began to lift and he felt more at peace within himself.

CHAPTER THIRTEEN

-

THE ~~DEVIL~~ EGO MADE ME DO IT

The ego is one of the main "characters" of the Course. On the surface, it appears to be the source of all our trouble, and we are encouraged to stop identifying with it, and choose a better teacher. The heavy use of metaphors in the Course makes it sound as though the ego were an actual individual who convinces us to do evil deeds. Many Course students, therefore, interpret the ego as *the new devil*, a demonic entity which makes us act against our will and best intent. But, the ego is actually just a thought in our mind; just like the Holy Spirit is, and both are really illusory.

In this chapter, we will discuss the ego, and explain how it gets its power. We will also examine how to weaken the ego, decrease our guilt and come to terms with its unreality. Finally, we will examine how our lives sometimes seem to get worse as we make progress in the Course, and we will see how to handle these situations. As usual, you will learn various hypnotherapy techniques to help you absorb and assimilate these ideas more easily.

The ~~devil~~ ego made me do it

THE NEW SATAN

Let's begin by briefly reviewing the origins of the ego (please refer to Part 1 for a more lengthy discussion). When the separation seemed to occur, two thought systems were created:

- The ego, which relished the autonomy it finally gained from God
- The Holy Spirit, which corrected the error and simply smiled at it, knowing nothing had really happened.

The mistaken perception that we separated from God led to guilt over our seeming sin; which led to fear that God would punish us for this sin. The world was thus created for us to "hide" in, and we (the Son of God) fragmented into billions of apparently separated entities. As we discussed in previous chapters, this is completely illusory, but until we fully and truly accept this to be true, we will continue to perceive a world of separation, in which "good" things and "bad" things happen.

As we read the Course, the two main *protagonists*, the ego and the Holy Spirit, *invite* us to follow their respective thought systems. By interpreting the Course with a Christian mindset, it's easy to view the ego as a demonic creature tempting us and deceiving us to fulfill its agenda and ensure its survival, and the Holy Spirit as the angel watching over us. By reading it literally, it is easy to misinterpret the nature of those two "entities". Since there are really no words to describe reality (i.e. our real Self), the Course uses metaphors and analogies to explain the principles it teaches. This is akin to a fairy tale or a children's book, in which amusing characters

150

and simple plots are used to form a story that a child can understand. This is the way we should consider the Course: it is written in language that will not create too much fear in us, and is adapted to our level of spiritual development. Just like a fairy tale, the Course addresses the spiritual infants that we are, in language we can comprehend. The ego and the Holy Spirit are not really two entities acting out the classic scene of good versus evil, but the familiarity of the story can help us understand its moral at a basic level, and for many, this is already great progress.

However, to avoid misinterpreting its content, it is important to remember the metaphysics of the Course and acknowledge its metaphorical nature. Instead of seeing the ego and the Holy Spirit as entities outside of us, exerting control over us, we need to remember there is nothing outside of the mind. So, it is better to think of them as two trains of thought in our split mind and recognize we alternate between them. Those thoughts are present in all of us, however dimly, and we all have the power to choose between them.

◆

So, what should our attitude towards the ego be? A total denial of its existence, even though true on level 1, would only be a self-deception. As long as we believe in its existence, we should have a healthy respect for the ego, and be vigilant to its lures. For instance, when you experience grievances, anger, specialness, etc., you should remember that you have a split mind, acknowledge you are currently perceiving the situation with your wrong mind, and that you have nothing to really be angry, guilty or fearful about.

The ~~devil~~ ego made me do it

Simply observe the situation without judgment. Say something to the effect of "here goes my ego again, up to its old tricks". By looking at the ego's ploy in a non-judgmental way, you slowly remove the fear that the situation created. You thereby remove its power since the ego is unreal and only has power as long as you believe in it.

The worst thing you could do is resist the ego and fight against it. This is exactly what it wants. By reacting to it in any way, you make it real, and therefore reinforce its power. Remember that the ego doesn't care if you love it or hate it, just that you pay attention to it. It does not care whether you are the biggest villain in the world or the kindest person in the world, as long as you are different (i.e. special), and feel that others are different from you.

Note that the biggest fear that people experience when going through this process is that they will lose their identity. And this is exactly what will happen in the end, but it is a very slow progressive process. After practicing this type of non-judgmental "observing", you will start to feel more peaceful and happy (what the Course refers to as the "happy dream"). But, this is not the end of the journey. Only after fully and truly accepting that the happy dream itself is an illusion will you finally go back home.

I have used the movie screen analogy earlier to describe the way we experience our life and I will use it again here in a slightly different way. The script is already written and you're watching the movie on the screen. How absurd is it then for you to get upset and angry at the movie, and start screaming at it or kicking the screen (especially considering *you* wrote

152

Hypnotic Spirituality

the script)? Continuing on that analogy, while in hypnosis:

1. Picture yourself sitting in the projection booth, watching yourself (dissociated) sitting amongst the crowd in the theater room below.
2. See yourself getting angry at the reaction of the "you" you are watching or judge yourself, and realize you're only making matters worse.
3. Now, instead sit in that booth, and observe yourself with Jesus (or whoever you see as your guide) by your side.
4. Smile and say "here goes my ego again".

This exercise is a type of dissociation that is very common in NLP (Neuro-Linguistic Programming), and made even more effective under hypnosis. Dissociation means literally "to disconnect". It is used to create some distance, to gain perspective, and therefore to see situations and yourself in perspective.

Dissociation techniques are helpful in dealing with conflict (allowing one to be more objective and to have better control of the situation) and monitoring oneself, and seeing oneself through the eyes of someone else. The outcome is usually that the person remains in control, feels fewer judgment-clouding emotions and learns from experiences.

This is a very good exercise to distance yourself from your ego reactions.

◆

A similar non-judgmental attitude should be practiced when you feel the need to use magic. Magic, as defined in the Course, is anything you do in the world to

153

The ~~devil~~ ego made me do it

alleviate perceived suffering (for instance, using medicine when ill or calling a friend when feeling lonely) or create pleasure (food, hobby, sex, etc.).

It is, of course, OK to do these things – the course does not prescribe or forbid any specific behavior in the world – as long as you are aware that it will not lead to salvation. It is just a temporary measure until you reach a point where you truly accept that they are not a source of healing (as the real healing is of the mind). Look without judgment at your ego choice to be sick (or lonely or whatever) and at your use of magic to "fix" it, and forgive yourself for thinking you are still a body and can experience pain or pleasure.

Unfortunately, many Course students misinterpret this aspect of the Course. They use this "non-judgmental looking" attitude as a way to luxuriate in their specialness, and to use the ego as an excuse for all their *sins*. "I can be as bad as I want to", they reason, "I'll just have to say that I'm looking at it with Jesus, and that it's the ego's fault." Unfortunately, this type of self-absolution does not lead to spiritual progress. Just saying the ego made me do it (a twist on the proverbial "the devil made me do it") is really a cop out, unless you really feel the implications of the choice you made. You need to be honest with yourself, and acknowledge when you are indulging your ego this way and luxuriating in specialness.

Engaging in specialness results in a lack of peace, and you need to be conscious of that, otherwise there would be no motivation to continue practicing the Course. You need to come to terms with the pain that comes from rejecting God's love. A good way to distinguish the ego's peace from Jesus' is that the latter includes everyone, whereas the former only includes a sub-group.

154

Hypnotic Spirituality

DAS GESTALT

Gestalt therapy is a form of therapeutic role playing. It is used to help release traumas by facilitating adult understanding at the subconscious level. It is frequently used when a client has been victimized by someone in the past (usually childhood). It can be conducted consciously or under hypnosis, but it is more effective under hypnosis, since the subconscious is directly involved and the conscious critical faculty is bypassed.

In this type of therapy, the client imagines himself talking to his victimizer (usually pictured sitting in a chair in front of him), then puts himself in that person's shoes and responds to the accusations. The two (victimizer and victim) keep swapping roles, thereby creating a dialog. The goal is for the client to get an understanding of the other person and what may have led to the abusive act.

The therapist sets the situation up so that the client feels safe telling the other person exactly how they feel about what happened (as a now-informed child). Then, a dialog is created with the client playing both parts. It is, of course, not recommended that the client imagine physically harming the other person.

The goal is for the client to forgive themselves as well as the person or situation in order to clear the event of its emotional impact. The truth of the actual event is less relevant. It's important to note that forgiving does not mean forgetting. The event happened and cannot be changed, but its emotional impact can. So, forgiveness in this context is for the client's benefit, not the perpetrator (who will always remain unaware).

The ~~devil~~ ego made me do it

If forgiveness is impossible at the moment, the next best objective is to reach an understanding and release, so that the client can still attain self-forgiveness.

 Here are a couples of ways that you can apply this technique to the Course:

1. Imagine the ego in the chair and role-play yourself and the ego in turns. This will help you understand the ego's motives and release the grudge you may feel against it. Forgiving the ego (or observing it without judgment) is a crucial step towards undoing it.
2. Another application of this method is to put the wrong-minded you in the chair and initiate a dialog with the right-minded you. This will result in you forgiving yourself for the times when you are in your wrong mind.

RESISTANCE

One of the biggest obstacles therapists encounter when working with clients is their subconscious resistance to change.

All our thoughts, habits and patterns of behavior come from previous subconscious programming from our parents, friends, schooling, the media, etc. This programming can be both positive and negative, but either way, once the subconscious has accepted it as true, it becomes very resistant to changing it. Part of the reason is survival. If some habit has resulted in our survival – and it has since we're still here – the subconscious will try to protect that habit to ensure

Hypnotic Spirituality

continued survival, even if the habit is actually not beneficial. The subconscious essentially strives to take us towards a feeling of comfort, familiarity and security, even if it's a destructive one.

A typical example is a woman who was abused and beaten by her father as a child, and who ends up in relationships with similarly abusive men. This choice of partner is obviously not in her best interest, but her subconscious finds in it a comforting familiarity.

Moreover, people get attached to their problems and identify with them. They may subconsciously resist any change for fear of losing that identity.

Finally, people may be reluctant to change because the change may require the need to take some action relating to various aspects of their life, and they will no longer be able to hide behind the fact that their "issue" is preventing them from accomplishing certain things. For instance, having a particular physical impairment may prevent a person from seeking work. And, they may be reluctant to take part in a trial for a miracle cure for fear of having to forever change the way they live their life.

◆

Whatever the reason for resisting change, the bottom line is that resistance is a major obstacle to healing. But, resistance does not mean that therapy cannot be successful. Because hypnosis bypasses the conscious critical faculty and allows access to the subconscious part of the mind, where negative programming resides, it is possible for this negative programming to be replaced with more beneficial behavior using positive suggestions. Regression styles of hypnotherapy, especially hypno-analysis, are also very useful in

The ~~devil~~ ego made me do it

allowing the subconscious to "let go" of old destructive patterns of behavior.

Similarly, the Course teaches us that all pain and struggles we experience in the world come from our resistance (to the Holy Spirit), a fear of the truth and a reluctance to "look through the eyes of Vision". This resistance is what makes *A Course in Miracles* so difficult to practice.

By learning how to look at situations without judgment (as described earlier), and forgiving yourself when you are unable to, you can greatly reduce the resistance.

EGO WEAKENING

It is very common for hypnotherapists to use a technique called "ego strengthening" during their sessions. Ego strengthening is basically direct suggestions aimed at increasing the client's confidence, self-worth and psychological strength: their "ego strength".

Note that, in this case, the word "ego" is used in its psychological meaning, not in the way *A Course in Miracles* uses it.

The original ego strengthening script was published by Dr John Hartland in 1966. It was considered revolutionary at the time, because it allowed for "brief" therapies - as few as 10 sessions as opposed to standard psychotherapies which often last 5 to 10 years. The originality of Hartland's Ego Strengthening script was that it aimed to strengthen the client, instead of weakening his symptoms.

158

Hypnotic Spirituality

The Text teaches us that the miracle restores the mind to fullness and shows us there is no lack in us. We are not aware of who we *really* are, and therefore feel a sense of scarcity. By showing us there is no lack in us, that we are the invulnerable Son of God, the Course in effect performs an ego strengthening therapy of sorts.

We can adapt the classic ego strengthening script for the purpose of the Course.

1. Imagine yourself as Christ, invulnerable, lacking nothing, and in perfect harmony with God.
2. Try to imagine what it would feel like.
3. Sense the strength in you that results from knowing you have everything and nothing can harm you
4. Picture a scene from everyday life
5. Transpose those Christ-like feelings to that scene.
6. Feel the peace that results
7. Repeat with a few more similar scenes (some pleasant, some unpleasant)

◆

The ironic part is that if we use the word "ego" as the Course uses it, the goal is to undo and *weaken* the ego until we are egoless. Note that this is a metaphor, the ego remains intact. We are just weakening its influence by spending more time in our right mind.

1. Induce a state of hypnosis
2. Picture an upsetting situation
3. Imagine the ego as a character of your choice, rejoicing at the event and waiting with glee for you to be upset and attack back

159

The ~~devil~~ ego made me do it

4. Watch yourself smiling at the situation and at the ego
5. See the ego lose *his* smile as he realizes that his ploy did not work
6. Repeat this with a few more everyday situations, noticing how the ego character seems to fade more and more with each scene

You can also use the theater metaphor described earlier.

1. Induce a state of hypnosis
2. Imagine yourself on the stage of a theater with the ego, playing a tragedy
3. Also picture yourself sitting in the audience, dissociated, looking at yourself.
4. Picture Jesus sitting beside you gently smiling at the scene
5. Don't try to change the scene
6. Don't judge or heckle yourself or the ego.
7. Just observe the scene, perhaps symbolically borrowing Jesus' glasses (or theater binoculars) in order to see the world as he does.
8. Think to yourself "Isn't my ego funny?"
9. See the tragedy turn to comedy as the ego exits stage left

YOU'RE SO SPECIAL...

Special love and special hate are two ways that the ego uses to keep us feeling guilty. Special hate involves finding scapegoats to blame for our issues and projecting our guilt onto them. Special love involves using another person to fill a perceived lack in ourselves. Note that the relationship can be with a person, a substance (drugs, alcohol, etc.) or a thing (money, fame, clothes, etc.). Ultimately, we should aim for what the Course calls holy relationships. See Part 1 for details on this subject.

The recognition of the type of relationship we're involved in is somewhat tricky. One way to tell is that a relationship is holy when it is at nobody's expense. Another hint is that special love always excludes people, whereas God's love is universal.

Hypnotherapy can help you set triggers that enable the detection of unholy relationships, raising your awareness of the fact that the relationship you are in excludes people or only favors one group. Follow a similar exercise to the one presented in Chapter 9.

In this case (as in every case), it's important not to judge yourself, otherwise you'd only be adding to your guilt. You just need to observe it, and recognize what you're doing. The Holy Spirit will take care of the rest once you ask Him.

THE EGO STRIKES BACK

As we make progress in the Course, it often seems like things are not necessarily improving for us in the world. As a matter of fact, things sometimes get worse. It's as if the ego takes offense at our spiritual progress, and strikes back at us to slow us down and discourage further progress. As a result, we fall sick, get attacked or some disaster befalls us.

It's crucial to realize that healing is of the mind, and does not necessarily materialize in any improvement in

The ~~devil~~ ego made me do it

form. If someone has cancer and they see their situation through the eyes of the Holy Spirit, they heal their mind, but it does not necessarily mean that their cancer will be cured. It may or it may not; and it does not matter. The healing that occurs in the mind is what matters. Even a fully healed mind may still fall victim to disease or attacks. Take Jesus as an example: he was clearly in his right mind, but you can't say that things were going too well for him in the world, especially towards the end of his life...

So, following Course practice to help stop wars, end world hunger, save the environment or otherwise make the world or yourself better is a misunderstanding of the Course's purpose. The famous line "Seek not to change the world, but choose to change your mind about the world" (T-21.In.1:7) should always be in your thoughts.

◆

So, the world (or you) will not necessarily get better because of your Course practice, but why do things actually get worse sometimes? Well, it's not so much that they get worse. They were bad to start with; we simply did not realize they were. Part of the Course's practice is designed to help us let go of our denial of how bad things are. This is why we spent the first chapter of this section focusing on this denial and getting to grips with the *awfulness* of the world.

As we start turning towards our mind (looking inwards rather than outside ourselves), what we see first is the hate of the ego. We need to go through that phase before we can experience true peace. In other words, if we are not aware of the hate within us, we will not know that there is a problem to fix. That's why a

Hypnotic Spirituality

large part of the Workbook encourages us to have an honest look at our mind, and acknowledge the hate in it. This may be painful for some, but is a necessary step, and the pain is only temporary.

The second reason that things can get worse is our subconscious (i.e. hidden) fear. As we make progress and get closer to *home*, part of us still does not want to return home. We subconsciously know that going home means losing our identity, and we are so attached to it that we may create a disease or some other disaster to sabotage and stall our progress. It's all right; the journey home can be slow and should not be rushed. It is crucial, however, for us to be aware of what is happening and to forgive ourselves for it. In a way, you can think of it as a measure of your progress.

In the great book "Feel the fear and do it anyway", Susan Jeffers advises us to get past our fear, as greater rewards await on the other side of the decision, and inaction due to fear is rarely the solution. We can follow this principle as well. Once we realize that our progress stalled because of unconscious fear, we can look at that fear in a non-judging way, and ask the Holy Spirit for help.

CHAPTER FOURTEEN

-

A PART OF ME

We all have various facets of our personality, and we all experience internal conflicts. We've all had internal debates where "part of me wants to do this, but part of me does not". For instance, does this sound familiar? "I want to accept this job because it pays better. Yes, but the commute will be longer. Yes but the benefits are better. Yes but I'll have to work long hours, etc."

This type of inner conflict is normal to some extent. But for some people, these conflicting aspects are so powerful that they negatively impact their lives. For many, these parts are so deeply hidden in the subconscious mind that they are totally unaware of their presence; and this is the problem.

In this chapter, we will discuss this phenomenon and the methods used in hypnotherapy to address the issue. We will also discuss how this applies to the Course and how to address issues at the spiritual level.

As usual, case studies will illustrate the topic and metaphors will be offered to help you absorb the concepts more easily.

A part of me

PARTS THERAPY

A typical example of conflicting parts is one of an obese man. A part of him wants to get rid of the weight, but another part wants to keep eating. The healthy part of him wants to be in good shape, and is in conflict with perhaps the child part who wants to pig out on sweets, or perhaps a part which is trying to create punishment for a past misdeed.

Please note that the type of conflicts described here do not represent Dissociative Identity Disorder (formerly known as Multiple Personality Disorder). The latter is a more serious condition, in which fully separate identities develop. These identities sometimes have different ages, genders, postures, gestures, ways of talking, even allergies. The inner conflicts that are referred to in this chapter are perfectly normal processes of a healthy mind, even though sometimes particular parts are misguided.

◆

Parts therapy is a hypnotherapeutic method that can very effectively aid in the discovery of conflicting parts. The therapist using this technique acts as a mediator. He starts by inviting various parts to come forward and identify themselves. The parts usually give themselves a name which gives an indication as to their function (e.g. "Protector"). For the more imaginative individuals, they can take the form of an animal or a fictional character.

The therapist then establishes rapport with all the parts. This neutrality is a critical part of the process, as the therapist is to remain impartial and listen to all the parts' views even the one(s) which, on the surface,

166

Hypnotic Spirituality

would appear to be detrimental. Indeed, all parts have the individual's best interest at heart, and influence the client's behavior out of good intentions. They just perceive the situation differently, and therefore prescribe different actions. By remaining neutral and objective, the therapist is able to create a non-judgmental environment, in which all parts feel free to express their opinions and become aware of the opinions of the other parts.

Parts therapy is similar to gestalt therapy (described earlier) in that it involves the client role-playing, but in parts therapy, they "play" all parts of their own personality instead of someone else's.

As each part expresses its view of the situation and the purpose for its actions, the other parts are encouraged to listen and respond respectfully to the stated position. In doing so, the therapist acts as a mediator or negotiator, helping each part understand the other's position, finding compromise, acceptance and resolution.

The therapist seeks terms of agreement between the parts, which often results in each part bending a bit. On occasion, a temporary agreement or partial resolution is agreed upon, with the goal of reaching a more permanent or complete one in a future session. Usually, this involves the problematic part taking on a new role, once it understands that what it had been doing is no longer serving any useful purpose.

Before closing the session, the therapist confirms the terms of the agreement, and verifies that all parts are satisfied with it. This is usually followed by suggestions to encourage confidence in the agreement and cooperation between the parts to carry it out. Next, the parts are asked to symbolically (and mentally) shake

A part of me

hands or embrace to seal the agreement, and merge back into an integrated whole, no longer at odds with each other.

Arianna's story

Arianna consulted for weight issues. She was very successful in her career as a lawyer, but was unable to get her weight under control. During a parts therapy session, two main parts came forward: one was named "Bouncer"; he described his role as a protector. When asked what he was protecting her from, Bouncer explained that, when she was young and slim, Arianna got into relationships with men who were only attracted to her for her looks, and treated her poorly, which resulted in abusive and traumatic experiences for her. The aim of this part was to make Arianna less attractive. By encouraging her to overeat and therefore carry more weight, Bouncer believed he was protecting her from such men, and therefore from further traumas. The second part called itself Jester, and he wanted Arianna to have fun, go out more, meet new people and be happy and healthy. A dialogue was encouraged between the two parts, so that they understood each other's concerns. They negotiated a compromise where Arianna would lose half of her excess weight, which would allow her to meet new men, but not the shallow kind that Bouncer wanted to avoid. Once in a loving relationship, she would lose the rest of the weight.

This is a typical scenario where both parts clearly had the client's best interest at heart and came up with a suitable compromise and a plan to move forward.

BILLIONS OF PARTS

In the context of *A Course in Miracles*, we realize that, even though we are one Son, different parts seem to have developed. They come in a wide variety of colors, sizes, shapes and personality types.

As a matter of fact, there are billions of them each acting seemingly independently, with their own ideas, prerogatives and agenda. The process followed in parts therapy can be paralleled to the process of joining. In this analogy, Jesus can be seen as the therapist. He listens to each part, treats them as if they were real and respects their views. He allows them to express themselves, without judging them or condemning them. But He reminds them they are part of a whole and encourages them to recognize their shared interests and guides them to join. This joining is, of course, in the mind as anything physical or worldly is an illusion.

YOUR OWN PARTS THERAPY

The other application of parts therapy to our practice of *A Course in Miracles* is to realize that we have two clearly obvious parts of our mind: the ego and the Holy Spirit. As we saw, most clients who undergo parts therapy are not even aware of the parts within them, and our first task is, under hypnosis, to identify and call out the parts involved with our client's symptoms. This is also a process that Jesus starts with in the Text and Workbook. He calls to our attention the fact that we have two parts within us. This comes as a surprise for most people, as we have repressed the "split" so deeply that we have become unaware of the parts.

Similarly to the parts identified in therapy sessions, both the ego and the Holy Spirit act with our best interest in mind. The ego argues "you wanted independence from God and here it is. You finally got what you wanted. Isn't it great?" It goes on and on about how great or awful the world is – it does not really matter to the ego which way you feel, as long as you believe it's real. The Holy Spirit is not quite as vocal. It just gently smiles, as It knows the unreality of it all. As the good therapist that He is, Jesus judges neither part, since condemning the ego would only make it real and reinforce it.

Instead he encourages us to acknowledge both parts in ourselves, to appreciate how they pull us in diametrically opposed directions, and to  realize that we oscillate between them constantly. This mere realization is tremendously therapeutic.

Over the course of the "therapy sessions", which for most people, take many lifetimes, we increasingly acknowledge our ego part, start to understand its ways and adopt the non-judgmental "smile-at-it" attitude of the Holy Spirit.

As in the parts therapy session, we eventually reach a resolution (Atonement) when we realize that the world has no meaning, and the ego part serves no purpose. At that point, just like the detrimental part of our client vanishes, the ego part's influence wanes as we align with the Holy Spirit's perspective.

IN PRACTICE

Applying this parts therapy method requires the individual to have a good theoretical understanding of right-mindedness and wrong-mindedness.

Also, given the interaction required and the need for a neutral mediator, I recommend working with a professional hypnotherapist to apply this method, instead of attempting to do it on your own.

The following is a description of such a session with Gloria, a Spanish lady, now residing in London.

Gloria's story

Gloria's understanding of the Course principles was very good, and she was able to very articulately describe the ego and Holy Spirit, but was struggling to makes sense of these two aspects in herself, and to reconcile the resulting conflicts. She was the perfect candidate for a parts therapy exercise.

After establishing hypnosis, I started the session by asking the ego and Holy Spirit parts in Gloria to come forth and identify themselves. Gloria was very creative and imaginative, and the parts were described as animal characters. The ego came first, and called himself Snake. This image is not surprising, but is in itself a judgment. The Holy Spirit part then came forth and called itself Dove. Again, a predictable figure, and also a judgment. But, such were her images at the moment, so I worked with them.

A part of me

I asked Gloria to let each part express itself. Snake spoke first, and started describing how great the world is, and all the pleasures it gives; then how unfair it is, and how she has been mistreated, casting judgment on other individuals or groups.

Dove spoke next, and countered Snake's arguments, striving to be inclusive instead of divisive, and argued the unreality of the world.

The session continued with this back-and-forth dialog. Gloria seemed to identify with both characters in turn, as was clearly evident based on her facial expressions.

We concluded the session with the parts acknowledging each other, which is a very promising step. Gloria described that, for the first time, she could clearly see the conflicting mindsets in her, whereas before she was just being subjected to them subconsciously, without being able to identify them. But, I knew we still had more work to do, as the symbolism of the parts (the snake and the dove) had been selected from a place of judgment.

Gloria was beaming when she came in for her next session. She said she had been able to better recognize in her everyday life when she was speaking like the "snake", and when she was acting like the "dove", and how this understanding helped her be less critical of herself and others.

I started the session by calling the parts out again. To my surprise (and Gloria's), Snake and Dove had now morphed into two vaguely-defined gaseous masses. Gloria described them as two clouds, one darker than the other. This was good progress, as the judgment initially felt had been reduced and the characters were more neutral.

172

Hypnotic Spirituality

The dark cloud was still promoting ego rhetoric, but interestingly, Gloria said its voice was a bit muted. When asked to speak, the white cloud remained silent. Being a diligent *Course in Miracles* student, Gloria sub-consciously knew that forgiveness "quietly does nothing.... It merely looks, and waits, and judges not" (W-pII.1.4:1,3); and this expressed itself in the white cloud's silence. This was definitely good progress and, this time, Gloria's facial expression remained peaceful throughout the session, even when the dark cloud was speaking.

As the session came to an end, I encouraged Gloria to have the two clouds symbolically embrace. She described the clouds moving towards each other, then the black cloud disappearing, and the white cloud vanishing as well, to leave a pure blue empty sky (Gloria's pictorial representation of the Atonement perhaps?)

Gloria seemed delighted with the experience as she was able to picture the two mindsets that drive her (and us all, for that matter) and symbolically visualize the Atonement. She felt she had made great progress in experiencing the Course, but humbly acknowledged she still had a long way to go before "truly" accepting the Atonement for herself. Don't we all?

173

CHAPTER FIFTEEN

-

I'VE GOT THE POWER!

A *Course in Miracles* is all about decisions: our decision to choose either the ego or the Holy Spirit as our teacher. In order to do this, we need to acknowledge we have a split mind and that we are better off choosing the Holy Spirit as our teacher. The previous two sentences are essentially a summary of the workbook.

Our mistaken decision to side with the ego and take the "tiny mad idea" seriously gets re-enacted in a multitude of situations, and we can choose to correct our mistake by seeing the world through the eyes of the Holy Spirit.

In this chapter,

- We will review the role of the "decision maker"
- You will realize that you do have a choice, and what the options are
- We will study cause and effect, and how your experience of each day is the result of the choices you made
- You will understand why you cannot make decisions by yourself
- You will learn how to correctly ask the Holy Spirit for help

I've got the power

As usual, the principles will be put into practice with hypnosis exercises and illustrated with a case study.

A SPLIT MIND IS A TERRIBLE THING

When the Son of God took the "tiny mad idea" seriously, it seemed He was able to separate from perfect Oneness (which is impossible, of course). The thought system of the ego was thus created, and it relished the newfound individuality. The correction came in the form of the Holy Spirit, which simply smiled at the idea and thought it silly.

At this point, we seem to have two antagonistic and diametrically opposed thought systems and a "decision maker" whose task is to choose between them. Note that when you read the Course, the "you" that it addresses is not the "you" you identify with in the world, but this decision maker that sits outside of time and space. Only decisions that occur at that level are meaningful.

The decision maker's choice to side with the ego engendered tremendous guilt, followed by fear of God's vengeance. The world was thus created as a place to hide, and the Son of God split into billions of fragments. In order to ensure its survival, the ego incessantly endeavors to convince us the world and body are real, and to keep us mindless. By doing this, the ego can rest assured that the decision is so repressed that we don't even know we have a mind capable to making another choice.

The power we have is in realizing we *do* have a choice, and can change our mind. We all share the same insane ego mind, the same sane Christ mind and the same decision maker who has the power to choose

Hypnotic Spirituality

between the two. Therefore, the ego's biggest fear is not of God or the Holy Spirit; it's of our *choosing* the Holy Spirit rather than itself as a teacher. Remember that the only force that has power over your mind is you (the decision maker). In a way, we can think of ourselves in this world as puppets (lifeless pieces of wood), which have no effect on the puppeteer (the decision maker). Only the puppeteer has the freedom to choose.

It's important to note that, on level 1, the concept of choosing is itself illusory. There is no choosing or free will in heaven because there are no alternatives to choose between.

THE CHOICE IS YOURS

We have discussed, in previous chapters, the futility of "doing" anything specific in the world. The only meaningful thing you can do in the world is to choose again. It sounds simple, but even realizing that you have a choice is not obvious. The original decision is buried so deeply that you are not aware of it. And that's exactly what the ego wants. This is why it tries to keep you rooted in the world. If you think you can find happiness outside of you (i.e. outside of your mind, in for example, vacations, careers, volunteering, shoes, purses, art work, charitable activities, hiking in the countryside, dining out with friends, sex, relationships, food, cars, gadgets, etc.), you are essentially re-enacting the original moment when you wanted to be independent from God, and were seeking a substitute for Him. That's why seeking pleasure outside will always lead to guilt. I'm not (and the Course is not either) advocating a life of chastity, privation and misery. You can still enjoy the

I've got the power

physical and psychological pleasures of the world, but realize that there's a part of you that chooses that over the peace of God. If you are aware of this, you won't feel guilty about it.

This is what the Course refers to as "magic". There's nothing wrong with using magic as long as you know that's what you're doing, and that it won't lead to your salvation. For instance, if you have a headache, it's OK to take a pill; and if you are lonely, it's OK to look for a companion. But, remember the problem is in your mind (outside of time and space), not in the world. Therefore, anything you do in the world will not really heal your mind. If you take your attention from the problem in the world and say "the problem is in my mind", you restore to your awareness that you have the choice. And, once you return to your mind, the right choice will be obvious (this is what terrifies the ego).

So, the purpose of the Course is *not* to not choose your ego (this is unrealistic for most of us), but just to be *aware* that you are choosing your ego. In other words, the goal of the Course is to make the unconscious conscious, that is to realize when you are following your ego, and then to look at it without judgment.

◆

So, how can we start developing this awareness? As we discussed in the chapter "Just an Illusion", you can start seeing the world as a shadow or a mirror of what is inside you. And if you do, that means there *is* an inside, therefore there *is* a mind, therefore there *is* a choice. This seems obvious and insignificant, but is the key to undoing the ego. Once you understand you have a split mind, the choice becomes meaningful. If you can learn

178

you made the wrong choice, you can realize there's another choice that can be made.

 We can expand on the projector-in-the-head analogy we used in Chapter 11 and add the notion of choice.

1. Induce a state of hypnosis
2. Picture yourself with a projector in your head and see the world around you as coming from it.
3. Imagine you have two filters you can place in front of the projector's lens: a green one and a red one.
4. Imagine a scene of everyday life projected out.
5. Place the red filter on the projector and see a world of separation, lack, attack and hate.
6. Feel the sense of unease that results from it.
7. Now, switch to the green filter.
8. The scene projected is still the same, but now you see it through the eyes of love and forgiveness
9. Become aware of the sense of peace that fills you.
10. Flip between the two filters and get in touch with the difference in the way you feel. It's a little bit like being at the optometrist, when he inserts all those lenses in turn and asks "Which is better? Lens A or lens B?"
11. Play with the filters and see how you feel, and become fully aware that *you* have the ability to choose which filter you want to use.

After repeating this exercise a few times, you should start to realize that the way you see the world is your own decision.

◆

I've got the power

Now that we have accepted that there is a choice, let's see what the choices actually are.

The ego's game is to keep you mindless so that the only choice you are aware of is between different forms of the ego dream. Do you want dream A or dream B? Do you prefer this illusion or that illusion? This is an illusory solution to an illusory problem.

In reality, the only choice is whether you want to be in or out of the dream. Make sure you understand the difference between what you think you want as an ego, and what you *really* want: to return home (which is of course where you really are, despite the ego continually trying to convince you otherwise).

At each instant, we're choosing between the ego and the Holy Spirit as our teacher (i.e. we're in our right mind or our wrong mind), but we are not aware of it consciously. We keep going back and forth. Remember throughout the day why you're here: to learn that you made the wrong choice and that you can make another one.

When confronted with problems or adversity in the world, instead of feeling that solving the problem in the world will bring you happiness, realize that the problem is the choice made by the decision maker. You can see the issue as a chance to make the right decision, where you had previously made a faulty one.

Choose the Holy Spirit as your teacher, and whatever you do in the world will automatically be the most loving thing.

Hypnotic Spirituality

DECISIONS, DECISIONS, DECISIONS....

Humility is the first step to making the right decisions. We tend to think that we know better than anybody else what the right actions in the world are. We're guided by social conditioning, "common" sense and accepted practices. We look at what happens and say "is it good for me, my family, my neighborhood, my city, my state, my country, my ethnic group, my religious group, my sports team, etc.?" But we cannot truly know what's good. What seems like a rational, sensible or even charitable choice in the eyes of the world may not be the most loving thing at all (and vice versa). In order to know what the best action is, you would need to know the entire history of the universe and everybody's Atonement path.

You are better off developing the humility that you do not know anything – think of yourself as a little child spiritually. The most important thing to understand is that you don't understand, and don't know how to listen (i.e. you don't know how to get your ego out of the way). If you think you already understand everything, you will not be open to being taught.

So, the first rule is to not make decisions by yourself (i.e. with your ego). Making a decision by yourself is a symbol of the original exclusion of God. Deciding by yourself will always hurt you; not so much the decision itself on the level of form, but the *thought* that underlies it will hurt you. Because it will reinforce the original thought of separation, you will experience the associated feelings of guilt and of deserving to be punished. The subconscious belief that God will punish you will create fear – manifesting in the world, for instance as the

181

I've got the power

unconscious fear that your boss, the stock market, the weather, etc. will punish you.

Since you don't know your own best interest (let alone anyone else's), the solution is to trust the Holy Spirit, ask for help and get your ego out of the way. First, look within at what the ego was trying to do and the investment it had in your specialness, and acknowledge you made the wrong choice. Then, simply ask Jesus or the Holy Spirit for help letting go of the interferences of the ego (judgments). This simple act of asking for help is the key to starting to undo the ego.

 Here, we can use an adapted version of the exercise presented in the "Back to School!" chapter.

1. Induce a state of hypnosis
2. Picture yourself as a kindergarten kid.
3. This is your first day in school, and you have much to learn.
4. Accept the fact that you don't know anything yet, and feel the eagerness to learn.
5. Imagine a scene from your everyday life
6. Transpose this feeling of humility and eagerness to learn to that scene
7. Say to yourself: "I am a spiritual infant who does not know or understand anything about the world. I need help."
8. Repeat for a few more everyday situations

Accepting you don't know anything and need help is a great first step, but you need to be careful *how* you ask for help and what you ask for.

WHAT'S YOUR PROBLEM?

What often trips us up when asking the Holy Spirit or Jesus for help is that we try to figure out the problem and ask for *specific* help. Instead of saying "I'm not at peace", we ask for specific fixes in the illusion (for instance with work, marriage, money, etc.), thereby reinforcing the error, and moving in the wrong direction. To make matters even more complicated, the problems are projections from within ourselves in the first place and are choices we made to reinforce our "innocent victim" mentality (see chapter "Face Lift" for details).

Therapists frequently see a similar pattern in their practice: clients exhibiting particular symptoms whose solution seems, at first glance, easy to fix. For instance, if someone is overweight, the obvious answer is to teach them proper nutrition, help them to stop overeating and design an exercise regimen that will help them shed the weight.

Hypnotic suggestions can be used to make eating healthy food a subconscious habit, and to motivate them to exercise. This works well in most cases, generally for people who are just a little overweight.

However, for more severe cases of obesity, there is usually an underlying cause that is much more deeply rooted. Indeed, the root cause is very individual, and in many cases, quite unexpected. Because each client's subconscious mind knows the cause of the issue, it always tries to do what it thinks is best for the individual, but this is sometimes based on faulty assumption. For instance, in the case of an overweight woman, it could be that she was abused as a child by a male family member. The memory of that event may be

I've got the power

repressed and hidden from the conscious mind, but the subconscious knows about it. In order to protect her from re-experiencing such trauma, it developed strategies to prevent the event from happening again. In this case, it means keeping men away and – in our society at least – most men are not attracted to obese women. "This", the subconscious reasons, "will keep us safe". This is obviously a flawed reasoning, and can be corrected once identified. Another possibility could be that the woman was a little chubby as a little girl. She loved being daddy's girl and he called her "my little puppy" in reference to her puppy fat. She got lots of attention from her father, which she did not ever want to lose. Therefore, her subconscious decided she should retain her "puppy fat" to continue this experience and the good feelings associated with it.

Another example could be of a male client who was told at a young age that he needed to eat everything on his plate so that he would grow up to be big and strong and able to take care of his own family one day.

In these cases, to really solve the issue, we would need to go back to the I.S.E. (Initial Sensitizing Event) using regression styles of hypnotherapy (see chapter 7 for details on these methods).

So, you see that the cause of a client's symptoms is not always obvious, and the client is better off letting the therapist guide them to uncover and heal the real cause of their issue. This is much more beneficial than trying to fix the surface symptoms. Similarly, we are better off letting the Holy Spirit heal our mind, where the real source of the problem is, instead of asking it to fix our illusory earthly "symptoms".

Hypnotic Spirituality

THE RIGHT WAY TO ASK

As a general rule, you want to refrain from asking the Holy Spirit for specifics. When asking for specific things, you are already telling Him what He should say. In other words, when asking for an answer, the natural tendency is to set it up so you hear the answer you want to hear. For instance, when you ask "should I move to city A or city B?", "should I take job A or job B?", "should I date Jenny or Diana?", "should I have fish or chicken for dinner?", you are trying to drag Jesus into the world you made up, and asking him to fix a problem in it. But how could He? If He did, it would confirm the world is real, and that there are indeed separate cities, jobs, women or dishes. By asking such specific questions, you are, in effect, reproducing the original attack, and attempting to control God all over again.

Be aware that the answer you hear from the Holy Spirit will not always seem to fix the problem the way you see it (i.e. by having your own needs met). Again, since we don't know the Atonement path of anybody, the answer may not seem to "make sense".

When asking for help, the real question is which teacher/advisor will you choose and how will you ask? Simply ask Jesus to help you look at the problem with you. Instead of asking for help with choosing between A and B, ask for help looking at the problem you *think* exists between A and B. This is more open-ended and does not reinforce the error.

◆

Now, a word of caution: we have to be careful not to confuse the ego's guidance and the Holy Spirit's. The ego

185

I've got the power

is sneaky, and will often masquerade as the Holy Spirit, answering questions in a way that, on the surface, seems sensible. So, how can we tell the difference? There is no sure way, but the following guidelines will help you determine the difference:

- First of all, just as it makes no sense to ask for specifics, if the guidance you are receiving seems to be specific, it is likely to be based on the ego.

- The ego is all about separation. We always look at the world in terms of what's best for us or our specific group. So, you know the ego is involved if you identify with only one side or group (e.g. when there is a terrorist incident). A true Holy Spirit answer will be good for the whole Sonship. It recognizes we are different in form or attitude, but we all share the same split mind: the insanity of the ego and the sanity of Holy Spirit. Any answer that does not have shared interest at its core is definitely ego-based.

- Love is your natural state. Struggle only comes because of the obstacles you place between yourself and love. When love is your source, everything is effortless. If you experience indecision or life seems a struggle, then the ego is likely to be involved.

- The Course is a non-dualistic philosophy, so be wary of any guidance that seems to indicate God knows about the world, does anything in the world

186

Hypnotic Spirituality

or asks you to change the world (or any similar hints of dualism).

- Finally, and perhaps most obviously, any form of specialness is a telltale sign of the ego's involvement. The ego doesn't care if you love it or hate it, just that you pay attention to it. Nor does it care if you are the best or worst person in the world, as long as you're different. So, in every answer, look for signs of specialness (good or bad).

Here's a little exercise to help you ask questions the right way (i.e. non-specifically).

1. Induce a state of hypnosis
2. Picture yourself at a game show.
3. In this show, you are asked a set of questions, and for each question, you are given four possible answers.
4. You also have the possibility to ask the audience for their opinion, and call a friend for advice. The nice thing is that you can use these options as many times as you want.
5. First, acknowledge you do not know the answers, and that you will be making use of these helplines on every question.
6. But here's the trick: you quickly realize that every time you ask the audience, their answer is inevitably one of the four multiple-choice answers... and is always wrong. You see, the audience members have their own agenda, and do not want you to win, so they always vote for the wrong answer. Therefore, no matter what they answer, you will be misguided.

I've got the power

7. Picture yourself asking for help choosing between the four answers, and following the audience's advice, and question after question, hear the host announce your answer is wrong.
8. Now, you can also call a friend for assistance. That friend (whose identity we will not reveal to preserve his privacy, but his name starts with J) has understood the game fully, and will wisely not pick a specific multiple-choice answer. As a matter of fact, you do not even have to read him the question or the possible answers. Instead, he inspires you to look at the question in the right way, and encourages you to let your heart guide you to the answer.
9. Repeat this for a few questions, and, of course, realize that the answer that comes to you is always right.

I HOPE I AM WRONG

The principles described above are simple (though the ego strives to convince us they are not), but not necessarily *easy* to implement. Most people understand (usually only at a subconscious level) that if they are wrong (i.e. the separation did not occur), following Course principles will lead to the undoing of the ego, and as a result, to the loss of their individuality.

Indeed, if the separation did not occur, the world does not exist and neither do we. We are so attached to our persona that the thought that we will "cease" to exist (and actually never existed at all) is terrifying, so we need to approach it slowly.

In the "Rules for decisions" section the Text (Chapter 30, section 2), Jesus gives a set of rules. These

Hypnotic Spirituality

are not sequential or linear. Since He knows people are at different stages of their spiritual development, He fully realizes that most of us will not follow rule # 1 (do not make decisions by yourself). So, the other rules are of the form "if you can't do that, perhaps at least you can do this..."

The first step is to have an honest look at your life, and how unhappy you are as a result of the decisions you have made. So, if you cannot side with Jesus at this point, at least realize that you're not happy and peaceful. In one of its most famous quotes, the Course asks "Would you rather be happy or right?" If you are honest with yourself, in most cases, you will say "right". Otherwise, you would not be here.

Once you acknowledge the unhappiness, you may start to accept that you *may* have been wrong, and therefore there *may* be hope. Indeed, if you feel bad but you think you've been right, then there's no hope. But, what if you were wrong? Then, there *is* hope! There may be a right answer somewhere. You can start thinking along the lines of "maybe someone knows better than I do and can teach me". By saying "I hope I am wrong", you open the door a bit. This is the "little willingness" mentioned in the Course, and this is all that is asked of you at this stage. This tiny grain of wisdom that you may be better off if you were wrong (or even just being open to the suggestion that you may be wrong) is the catalyst for further progress.

This is what the miracle does: it leaves the door open to the possibility that you were wrong, and it brings to your awareness the fact that you can make another choice. You now have hope because you know the mind can choose again, and choose rightly this time. But, the

189

I've got the power

miracle does not make the choice for you; *you* have to make that choice.

Then comes gratitude: "Thank goodness, I was wrong (about everything) and there's someone who can guide me and help me". This is a course in developing humility and gratitude.

BE CAREFUL WHAT YOU WISH FOR...

In the "Rules for Decisions" section, the Course also describes the cause and effect relationship between our decision and the type of day we will have.

The conventional (ego) logic is that what you feel is based on the way the situation turned out. That means you're at the mercy of forces beyond your control. In other words, the dream is *dreaming you*.

In contrast, the Course's view is that, since the world is a projection of what's inside your mind, you first tell yourself the kind of day you want, the things you want to happen to you and the feelings you want to experience, and situations will materialize so that these feelings are experienced. In other words, *you* decide what you want: a day of peace or a day of conflict.

So, if you're upset right now, it's because you *wanted* to be upset and didn't want the peace of God (as it would eventually lead to your disappearance). It's not evil, it's not sinful, it's just silly.

So, ask yourself if you want conflict and anxiety or forgiveness and peace. The outcome of events will depend on what you chose at the beginning. By outcome, I don't mean the specific outcome of a meeting, date or event, but whether you will feel more guilty, anxious and special or more peaceful. In the ego's world (the one we

190

Hypnotic Spirituality

are most familiar with), it's the reverse – the outcome is dependent on the situation.

So, if you feel any kind of discomfort, it's because of your choice to be with the ego. And that's all right (no need to feel guilty about it). The reason you don't want to forgive is that you don't want the peace that comes from it. And the reason you don't want this peace is that it would mean the end of your specialness and lead to the end of your individual identity.

Therefore, if you hold on to grievances, realize that it's because you basically decided "I want a day of conflict". And that's all right, as long as you are aware of it. In general, the reason you feel miserable is because you've chosen to feel that way and made it your goal. If your goal is to be a victim, you will go around looking for people to victimize you or reject you, and you will experience what you wanted to. Next, you forget that you set the goal in the first place, so you don't realize that what happens to you is your choice. And the events and situations that occur seem like unfair attacks against you.

Similarly, if you're upset, it's because you chose to be, but instead of accepting responsibility, you project it onto someone or something else and say "the reason I'm not happy is because of XYZ".As long as XYZ is outside of you, you know you are listening to the ego. The problem is not the specific situation, but the goal you chose. Once you realize you have chosen this, look at it with Jesus and gently smile at it, instead of looking at it with your ego (i.e. judging yourself).

Here's a simple exercise that will help you practice this principle.

191

I've got the power

1. Induce a state of hypnosis
2. Recall a recent event from your life when you were upset, angry, depressed, etc.
3. Imagine you are watching it on a TV screen, and replay that scene.
4. Play the scene backwards at a fast speed and continue rewinding until you reach that morning when you woke up.
5. Picture, on your night table, two cards: one reads "Upset" and the other "Peace".
6. See yourself picking the "Upset" card
7. Fast forward to the upsetting scene and feel the upset.
8. Rewind one more time to the morning, but this time, pick up the "Peace" card.
9. Fast forward one last time to the end of the scene, and see yourself very peaceful despite the situation that just occurred.
10. Repeat this exercise for several recent upsetting situations.

CHAPTER SIXTEEN

-

WHOSE LIFE IS IT ANYWAY?

In Part 2, I described Past Life Regression, the process used to take someone back to explore previous lives under hypnosis (please refer to Chapter 7 for details on this approach).

In this chapter, we will review this therapeutic technique briefly, and discuss how it can be applied in the context of *A Course in Miracles*. Note that the Course does not directly discuss re-incarnation, but it is implied in that it states the Course saves "a thousand years of time as the world judges it".

We will also see how we identify with our current persona and how to get past the fear of losing it. This is indeed a crucial step to any spiritual progress, as the resistance to the idea of losing one's identity is the major obstacle to accepting our "return" to the Oneness of God.

Whose life is it anyway?

IT'S MY LIFE

Let's first review briefly the concept of Past Life Regression (PLR). In a typical PLR, the client is guided into a fairly deep state of hypnosis and taken back in time, in a fashion similar to current life age regression. But, depending on the client's reasons for wanting to experience a PLR, he is invited to go back to a life and an event that is relevant to his issue, or to a life that he would find most beneficial at this time. This is obviously only applicable if the client believes in re-incarnation, and it's not the goal of the therapist to try to convince him if he does not. When a current issue originates in a previous life, as was the case for Bill (see the case study, in the PLR section of Chapter 7), the revivification of the initial sensitizing event (i.e. the cause) will generally lead to rapid and complete healing of the current condition.

Whether someone seeks a PLR purely out of curiosity or to attempt to resolve a current issue that may have originated in a previous life, there is always some excitement, occasionally mixed with a little fear, similar to what is experienced when embarking on a journey to an unknown land. But there's one major difference: not only is the land unknown, but your identity is unknown as well. This, in my opinion, is the reason why a PLR can be a hugely beneficial spiritual experience. People suddenly find "themselves" in a lifetime quite different from their current one, perhaps as someone from a different race, gender, country, religion, etc. Quite often, this comes as surprise to some and a shock to others, as in that past life, they may discover that they belonged to a group they despise today. By becoming aware that their current persona and body are nothing more than a

194

Hypnotic Spirituality

temporary vehicle through which they can experience the lessons of the world, the level of prejudice in the individual is reduced substantially.

This, in my opinion, is a crucial step in acknowledging the true Christ nature in everyone you meet. Indeed, with the knowledge that you were all these different people in the past and once you are able to accept this without judgment and still love yourself, you can extrapolate that love to all people you meet who look like the "you" of those past lives. As a matter of fact, you can gradually start seeing everyone as a different incarnation of you.

This naturally leads to joining, since you more readily accept the shared Christ nature of everyone around you and begin to focus on shared interests.

Past Life Regressions (like other forms of regression) are very interactive sessions, where you "explore" under the guidance of the therapist. Therefore, it's not something you can easily do on your own.

To benefit fully from this experience, I recommend you seek a hypnotherapist trained in PLR. Please see the "Resources" section at the end of this book for sites that list such therapists. Now, since your therapist may not be familiar with Course concepts, I suggest you add (in your mind; you do not have to verbalize it) the feeling of "joining" with yourself in each life that you recall. This will help you join with others in this life.

Here are a couple of exercises you can do on your own to help come to terms with the many faces you have taken over time.

195

1. Induce a state of hypnosis
2. Imagine yourself flicking through a huge photo album. This is the photo album of your life; each picture is of you at different ages in different situations.
3. The peculiar thing is that, in each picture, you look different.
4. Notice that, as you flip the pages, you are in turn white, black or Asian, male or female, rich or poor, victim or oppressor, etc.
5. Make sure you include happy scenes and tragic ones and everything in between.
6. For each scene, take a moment to truly identify, in your mind's eyes, with the person in the picture.
7. Whatever the images, simply note each scene without judgment.

Here's a variation on the same theme.

1. Picture yourself reading the newspaper.
2. Read through various stories, some happy, some tragic.
3. All stories are illustrated with photos of the individual involved.
4. As you look at the photos, you realize that your face is on every character: the murderer who killed 3 people last week, the dictator from a foreign land, the fireman who rescued the cat from the tree, etc.
5. All these individuals, all their victims and all people associated with the story have your face.
6. Keep flicking through the newspaper and associate with each character in turn.
7. Again, read each article without judgment.

Hypnotic Spirituality

THANKS FOR THE MEMORY

Our conscious memory is quite small and mostly short term. We only remember a handful of things on immediate recall. However, our subconscious mind remembers every moment of our life in great detail, which can allow a hypnotherapist to uncover his client's ISEs (Initial Sensitizing Events) and events that had been repressed and hidden from the conscious mind (see Chapter 7 for details).

Occasionally, hypnotherapists see clients who have misplaced a valuable object. They may have hidden it to protect it from being stolen, but then completely forgotten where the "safe place" was located. Under hypnosis, it is possible to help them access these memories and "relive" that part of their life when they last had sight of the object. The subconscious mind is so full of information that the police have also used hypnosis to help witnesses recall specific details of a crime scene (such as a license plate number) that they could not consciously remember.

◆

I personally believe that we actually have access to even more memories than those related to "our" lives (past or present). Since we're not really separate at the level of mind, there's no reason why our memories should be limited to a particular lifetime or body. In each of our minds, we have the entire history of the ego (i.e. the universe). Quantum scientists have proven the existence of a "field" that contains this information in a hologram-like structure. *The Holographic Universe* and *The Field* (see recommended reading section) are

197

Whose life is it anyway?

excellent books on the subject and provide a detailed description of this theory.

At any moment, we choose to experience part of the hologram. It's like tuning to a different TV channel (it could be ancient Greece or 200 years in the future).

Though, to my knowledge, no formal experimentation has been done, I believe that, if one were to go deep enough in hypnosis, he would be able to access some of this information and experience any part of any lifetime in the history of the universe. And this is, in my opinion, exactly what happens during past life regressions. The individual "tunes in" to a particular channel and accesses the memories of *some* lifetime. It is irrelevant whether it is his own or someone else's since we are one anyway. The memory that is tuned into will have direct bearing on the issues the person is having. As we discussed earlier, in the same way that free association (see Chapter 7) allows the client to access memories that appear random but are actually very much related to the cause of their issue, past life regression subjects will access a "life" and a set of memories that will help them understand and heal their current life issue.

Moreover, since time is an illusion and we have access to all the memories of the universe – past, present and future – there's no reason why the "past" life tuned into would have to be in the past. It should be equally possible that people find themselves as a space trooper on a futuristic planet, rather than a peasant in the middle ages. It's just their limiting beliefs of time linearity that prevent them from accessing these "future" memories. This hypnosis technique is not as common as PLR and is sometimes referred to as "future life progression".

198

Perhaps, we may even be able to reach memories of the (seeming) creation of the universe when separation appeared to happen. A glimpse at that instant would, no doubt, be an excellent learning experience.

Here's an exercise that attempts to reproduce this event.

1. Induce a medium state of hypnosis
2. Picture yourself standing on a long, bright, shiny, straight line extending in front of and behind you as far as the eye can see.
3. Picture yourself floating over the line and start to drift along it.
4. As you drift slowly back, you see sign posts with pictures of your past.
5. As you continue, you see pictures of historical events: World War II, the American Civil War, the French Revolution, the Renaissance, the Middle-Ages, the time of Jesus, ancient Egypt, etc.
6. You continue your journey and see scenes of cavemen and dinosaurs, then the earth in its early days when it was just formed, then the creation of our galaxy and other galaxies. Until you reach the "Big Bang".
7. Float past the explosion and see yourself right after the tiny mad idea "happened". You are standing (as the decision maker) with the ego on one side and the Holy Spirit on the other, weighing both sides.
8. Continue observing the scene (without judging yourself) as you make the choice for the ego.
9. At this point, start moving forward through time and you see the universe being created.
10. Slowly float back to today, through all the events in history, and land back on the line where you started,

Whose life is it anyway?

thrilled to have witnessed such a "momentous" event as you now fully understand the impact of that decision and the unreality of all that was to follow.

A THERAPY OF MANY LIFETIMES

It generally takes a series of hypnotherapy sessions to heal a client's issues. It should always be remembered that the past and situations that occurred cannot be changed, but it is possible for clients to change the way they feel about these things. The Course says "Seek not to change the world, but choose to change your mind about the world" (T-21.In.1:7). As described earlier, revivification of past events can help clients see situations differently. The past event hasn't actually changed. The emotions and meaning that the client attached to the event have been released and it is this that leads to healing.

As Course students, our aim is to release our guilt (or realize its unreality), which will in turn enable us to return home. When we learn to forgive one type of situation or person and not let it upset us, part of our mind is healed and that lesson does not have to be learned again. Our "work" flows over from one lifetime to the next until we are fully healed and can, at last, let go of the thought that we are separate and just remember we are peace and love.

So we can think of each life as a therapy session, and we should seek to make the most progress possible in each session. Yes, you could choose to delay some of the lessons to another life, but why wait? Why carry the pain that comes from unhealed guilt any longer than you have to? Let's take every opportunity to learn the lessons offered to us.

Hypnotic Spirituality

IDENTITY CRISIS

Quite often, our clients have identified with their problem. They have gotten used to being a "sufferer of XYZ". Such a condition usually comes with "benefits" (therapists call them "secondary gains") such as attention, pity or sympathy from others. Despite the apparent pain they endure and their stated desire to get better, they secretly luxuriate (often unconsciously) in their state and identify fully with it.

Secondary gains are a major reason why therapy sometimes fails to produce long term results. The client has subconsciously identified with his issue, and is terrified at the idea of losing that identity. The reasoning probably goes something like this: "if I'm not a XYZ sufferer, I will not be myself anymore, since this is who I am". Therefore, the subconscious will sabotage efforts to get better.

The parallels with *A Course in Miracles* are obvious: we are here because of the individuality we sought. We identify with this body, and despite the terrible conditions we may be in, we still choose the individuality. The concept of pure Oneness is a terrifying prospect, and therefore we sabotage the attempts at reaching it.

So, even though we may understand the solution to our problems on an intellectual level, we are afraid of it because it will ultimately lead to the end of the ego, and therefore our disappearance.

◆

Hypnotherapy techniques can help us disassociate from our worldly identity and be more aware of our true

201

identity as Christ. By realizing that the former identity is an empty shell, destined to suffer in this world, and our real identity is one of bliss, lacking nothing, it becomes much easier to gradually release our attachment to the outcome of any situation in the world and our earthly form.

Try the following exercise:

1. Induce a state of hypnosis
2. Picture yourself as you are today, looking at yourself in a mirror.
3. Slowly see the image in the mirror morph into another face. It could be someone you know or an imaginary face.
4. Repeat this several times, realizing that the face (and by association the personality) you are used to is not really your true self.
5. Conclude the exercise by seeing the face in the mirror slowly fading and being replaced by a blinding bright light (symbolizing your true Christ nature).

CHAPTER SEVENTEEN

-

JUST UNDO IT!

Even though all spiritual paths lead (back) to the same place in the end, *A Course in Miracles'* claim is to assist us in getting there faster than other paths (and certainly faster than on one's own). By showing us the way to achieve the undoing of our ego, and providing very practical workbook lessons, it helps us realize the world is an illusion, come to grips with our oneness and practice forgiveness. Following the teachings of *A Course in Miracles* is said to symbolically save 1,000 years (i.e. many lifetimes) in our spiritual progress.

But, as clear as the message of the Course is, and as much as people are willing to practice it, it is very difficult to make it a long-term habit and rid ourselves of the "baggage" that is in the way of our progress.

Our subconscious mind is powerful, and can either hinder or help us. Hypnotherapy has well developed techniques to help in this area, and I contend that applying them will save you even more lifetimes.

In this chapter, we will make use of several of the hypnotherapy techniques discussed previously, and apply them to help undo the ego by firmly embedding Course practices and teachings into the subconscious

Just undo it!

mind. In this way, our subconscious will begin to automatically make the right choices with significantly less resistance.

As the Course says, "the miracle does nothing. All it does is to undo. And thus it cancels out the interference to what has been done. It does not add, but merely takes away." (T-28.I.1:1-5,8)

MAKE IT A HABIT

Miracle principle number 5 teaches us that "Miracles are habits and should be involuntary. They should not be under conscious control. Consciously selected miracles can be misguided."

By using the word "involuntary", this principle tells us that we should not attempt to perform miracles consciously, but let the Holy Spirit perform them. Our only task is to *choose* the Holy Spirit's guidance. And by "habit", it means that it should be an automatic process (i.e. at the subconscious level) for us to seek this help.

So, when we get upset or angry at someone, instead of trying to fix the problem, we should make it a habit to ask the Holy Spirit for help in changing the way we perceive the person or situation.

It is easy to say to "make it a habit", but breaking bad habits (whether they be smoking, overeating, biting one's nails or an ego-driven behavior) and setting good habits is one of the most difficult things for people to do consciously. It can sometimes be done through sheer willpower and/or repetition, but it is difficult, takes time and there is always the potential to slip back into old ways.

204

Hypnotic Spirituality

Fortunately, this is an area in which hypnotherapy excels, as it can help implant new habits and behaviors and override bad ones. This is achieved by offering these new ideas to the subconscious while in a state of hypnosis. This directly "implants" these positive suggestions into the part of the mind that controls our habits and behaviors – which drive us – and teaching it that the habit that it's keeping (though possibly well-intentioned, and maybe even initially positive when the habit started) is not to the benefit of the client. As discussed in previous chapters, by also installing triggers, it is possible to increase conscious awareness of wrong-minded thoughts so that forgiveness can take place.

Applying this to the Course, you can learn to react to upsetting situations with amusement rather than judgment.

1. Induce a light state of hypnosis
2. Think of a situation when you got angry or upset
3. Recall how, as a "good" Course student, you subsequently felt guilty about your reaction.
4. Picture that situation, vividly and repeat in your mind "Here goes my ego again" and smile internally.
5. Repeat this with a few scenarios.

Sally's story

Sally, a 33 year-old nurse from Essex, England was an avid Course student. She had diligently read the Text, completed all the Workbook lessons and read the

205

Just undo it!

Manual for Teachers. However, she was frustrated by her apparent lack of progress. During the consultation, she recounted how many times she would get angry at things or people and, despite knowing better, she would then get upset at herself later for having gotten angry. Of course, this only made the error more real and led to more guilt, which aggravated the situation even further.

The therapy sessions were not designed to prevent her from being angry, but to break the habit of beating herself up for it afterwards. Using triggers, I helped Sally install a new habit instead: looking at her recent anger without judgment, with a smile, and the statement in her mind "here goes my ego again". Over time, she reported that she still got angry at times (though less often), but when she did, it did not affect her like it used to. She could take a step back and look at her ego in action and remain serene about the experience.

SAY THAT ONE MORE TIME!

A Course in Miracles is a lengthy book, but it can be distilled down to a few simple principles. The reason the Course is so long is that it repeats its teachings over and over. Instead of being a linear logical progression – as is common in teaching methodologies – the Text circles back over and over the same ideas in a symphonic way, so that they sink in a little more each time. Similarly, the Workbook seems to come back to the same points, and has several review periods. Even within a given lesson, the verbiage is very repetitive, and we are asked to repeat several times a day (sometimes once an hour) the affirmations of the day.

Hypnotic Spirituality

The principles taught are so at odds with all that we believe to be true in the world that it's impossible to adopt them right away. As described in Chapter 5, our Conscious Critical Faculty (CCF) acts as a valve that prevents information contrary to that which has already been established as true to permeate through. But over time, with constant repetition and a little willingness, the ideas will eventually begin to sink in. It just takes a long time.

Hypnotherapy, on the other hand, bypasses the CCF and establishes selective thinking. This allows the therapist to circumvent the regular critical process and implant new ideas that will take root in the subconscious.

An analogy would be trying to reach an underground water stream that is buried under 300 feet of hard rock. To get to it, you can take a hammer and chisel and start chipping away at the surface. Over time, you will reach the stream but it will take a *long* time. But, what if you could bypass the hard rock stratum, perhaps going further out a little, where the soil is soft and easy to dig, or better yet, go to the stream before it gets underground and simply float down. You would, obviously, reach your goal faster.

In a similar way, by talking directly to the subconscious, hypnotherapy can help you achieve the goals of the Course faster and with fewer repetitions. I'm not suggesting you skip the Text or the Workbook. But, adding hypnosis techniques as a learning tool will greatly speed up your acceptance of its teachings and allow you to make faster progress.

207

Just undo it!

KEEP IT REAL

We all know that forgiveness is at the core of the Course's teachings. However, the word "forgiveness" is often misinterpreted. What the world typically considers forgiveness is really not a genuine form of forgiveness, since it considers the sins real and decides to only ignore or forget them. This is what I call fake forgiveness, or "forgiveness-to-destroy" as the *Song of Prayer* (a supplement to the Course) puts it.

Be honest with yourself regarding the reasons why you may feel compelled (or sometimes coerced) to forgive. You, most likely, truly feel you have been harmed or wronged by someone (i.e. you believe the sin against you is real). In so doing, you reinforce the belief in separation: there is a sinner and a *sinnee,* a forgiver and a *forgivee.* And the people who wronged you deserve to be punished for their sins. However, in order to prove what a "good" person you are, you will overlook their sins. God will surely notice your innocence and benevolence, and grant you heavenly brownie points. So, a lot of what passes as forgiveness in this world is really more concerned with self-interest than the interests of others (i.e. joint interests).

◆

The Song of Prayer describes several ways in which this fake forgiveness manifests itself (S-2.II.2-6). These can be summarized as follows:

- Superiority: I am more righteous than you are and, in my *grandeur,* I consent to overlook the misdeeds of this miserable sinner.

- Reciprocity: I'm just as much of a sinner as you are, so I'll let you off the hook because I'd like to be let off the hook too.

- Martyrdom: I submissively accept the suffering you inflict on me, so that God will notice and reward me for my sacrifice.

- Conditional: I may forgive you if you apologize, repent or show regret for your sins or make it up to me in some way.

All these have one thing in common: the belief in the reality of the sin and the conviction that you have been wronged. Fake forgiveness is a brilliant part of the ego's plan, where by masquerading as a good deed, it manages to make the world of separation more real and subtly reinforce our guilt.

So, it is pretty clear that this fake forgiveness is counterproductive and only serves to reinforce the ego.

◆

So, what is "real" forgiveness? By reminding yourself of your Christ nature, you remember you are sinless and cannot be harmed. Therefore, the "sin" against you can only be a misperception. Why would you then feel someone deserves punishment? By recognizing the Christ in you as well as in the "offender", you reveal the unreality of the sin, and share in the innocence and love that is your true nature.

Practicing real forgiveness is a sure way to undo the ego. Easier said than done, of course. In order to switch

Just undo it!

from fake to real forgiveness, the first step is to start recognizing when you demonstrate fake forgiveness (in any of the forms enumerated above).

As usual, strive to not feel guilty when you catch yourself practicing fake forgiveness and forgive yourself for it. But, how can we ensure that the forgiveness we practice is real and not ego driven? By asking help from the Holy Spirit, the symbolic representation of true forgiveness.

1. Under hypnosis, picture a situation where you felt wronged or harmed by someone, and who you later decided to forgive.
2. Replay the "wrongdoing" in vivid details,
3. See yourself forgiving that person.
4. Dig deep into the true motives of the forgiveness, and do your best to identify any of the four patterns described in the Song of Prayer (superiority, reciprocity, martyrdom or condition). Be honest with yourself.
5. Picture a light coming into the picture (representing the Holy Spirit) and ask for help in "really" forgiving.
6. See the light envelop the offender and reveal his true Christ nature.
7. See that light emanating from you as well, revealing *your* Christ nature.
8. With the whole picture now bathed in light, replay the scene where you were wronged and realize the absurdity of seeing that "sin" as real.
9. Smile gently at the situation as you acknowledge your misperception.
10. Repeat this exercise for a number of similar situations.

Note

With this type of therapy, I diverge from most conventional hypnotherapists and psychotherapists, who encourage their clients to accept that the "sin" has indeed happened, but since there's nothing they can do about it, they might as well let it go and forgive the offending party, thus releasing themselves from the negativity.

Although this provides great relief for people who are hurting themselves by holding on to grievances, I suggest that Course students take it one step further by realizing the unreality of it all.

THE SOUND OF SILENCE

Many spiritual paths encourage their followers to quiet their mind, silence the "monkey chatter" or simply be still. Similarly, the Course exhorts us to provide "a silent invitation to the truth to enter, and to make itself at home...For what you leave as vacant, God will fill, and where He is there must the truth abide." (T-27.III.4:1,3)

Some people interpret such statements literally, as meaning we should vow to not talk anymore. Or, they assume it means isolating oneself from all aspects of the world by meditating, or using hallucinogenic drugs. But, as usual, it is not what we actually do or don't do and say or don't say in the world that matters, but what happens in the mind.

What the Course means by silence (or stillness) is the peace that fills you when you see past the illusions of the world. So, by encouraging you to be still, quiet or silent, the Course is really reminding you of your true nature as Christ. By realizing nothing in the world can hurt you or

Just undo it!

affect you, the constant flow of worries, fear, regrets, guilt, etc. ceases. And, this happens at the level of the mind. Therefore, it can happen in the midst of chaos, while appearing normally active in the world.

Meditation is a common way people attempt to apply the stillness principle. Meditation is not specifically required as a practice in *A Course in Miracles,* but it does not discourage it either if people feel it will help them. However, it needs to only be considered as a tool, a means to an end, to get a sense of what stillness is and be able to apply it in other situations.

I need to caution against the temptation to treat meditation practice itself as holy, and turn it into a ritual or an idol. Like with any other rite (religious or otherwise), many people practice meditation as a daily routine (almost a chore sometimes) that they feel they *have to* do, in order to be a "good" person. And that in itself, they're convinced, is contributing to their enlightenment. This is another subtle ploy of the ego to convince them they are holier than others because they perform certain actions. And this is, of course, a form of specialness. Always remember that the purpose of your actions should be to undo the ego. You could be isolating yourself in a cave, making vows of silence, or breathing deeply standing on your head for a year, it would not make a difference to your enlightenment if you still believed in separation and the reality of the world.

So, this is what silence is: an open mind, which freed of all the obstacles to love's presence and of the beliefs in separation, will automatically be filled with God's peace. Once this peace has filled you, it will extend to all others you come in contact with; once again, not through any specific action or words, but through your mere state of mind. As the Text says, "you need do nothing"

212

Hypnotic Spirituality

(T-18.VII), meaning you just need to remove your concerns for the world and your worries of what to do, and this will create the "quiet center" (T-18.VII.8:1-5) to receive God's peace.

As usual, quieting the mind and letting go of concerns is a gradual process. Do not be too harsh with yourself if you cannot achieve it fully. Be gentle with yourself and forgive yourself for having a split mind.

CLEARING THE FIELD

As we discussed in Part 1, hypno-analysis helps clear out emotional blocks accumulated during this life, and that are holding people back. These accumulated issues can also stifle spiritual progress and make applying the principles of the course even more difficult.

Of course, hypno-analysis sits in the illusion and does not purport to provide true healing as the Course describes. But, for those people whose life is so troubled they cannot make measurable progress, this can be a very beneficial first step.

Hypno-analysis has the additional benefit of allowing repressed memories to rise to the surface so that emotional release occurs along with healing. As a result, people who have repressed traumas can benefit greatly from this technique. Indeed, how can you forgive yourself and others for your "victimization" if you are not even aware of it?

CHAPTER EIGHTEEN

-

A NEW PROPHET

In this chapter, we will look at the notion of "prophet" and what, I believe, is its equivalent in terms of the Course: the Teacher of God. You will learn some exercises and hypnotherapy techniques to help you be a better teacher, thereby helping those around you be aware that they too can make another choice.

PROPHET OR TEACHER?

The word "prophet" is widely misunderstood and carries obvious religious connotations. Etymologically, it comes from the Greek *prophetes,* where *pro* means "before" and *phetes* means "speak". Therefore, it roughly translates to a foreteller, one who can see and speak of the future.

A meaning closer to the original Hebrew word would be "one who speaks for someone else". The exact definition and powers attributed to prophets vary by culture and religion, but the common theme is that they convey messages of divine inspiration. In that sense, we can see the prophet as a proxy for God (whoever God is for the particular culture), one who can translate into

A new prophet

words that we can understand what is essentially indescribable; a conduit through which God could address a particular people.

We are all aware of the famous prophets: Moses, Isaiah, Jesus, Muhammad, etc. But, there are countless others who were similarly inspired, but did not leave their mark on history. Considering prophecy as a channel for divine inspiration would allow one to include in the list people such as Shakespeare, Mozart or Leonardo da Vinci, as their message was inherently divine and expressed through their respective art form.

My own definition of a prophet is someone who is in his right mind often enough that the love of heaven gets reflected on earth in one form or another. It's as if a tiny prick of light shined through a small hole in the darkness and lit up one fragment of the Sonship.

We actually all possess this light in us and oscillate constantly between right-mindedness and wrong-mindedness, between the ego's mindset and the Holy Spirit's. When in our right mind, we reflect heaven's love and our actions in the world become the most loving thing to do in the particular situation. This is how, for instance, the Course came about. This metaphorical light of heaven shined on Helen, which put her in her right mind, and allowed her to scribe the Course.

So, in my opinion, a prophet, in the purest sense of the word (i.e. a proxy for God), is the equivalent to what the Course terms a "teacher of God". This teaching is love reflected in this world in various forms – be it a speech, a play, a book, a symphony, a sculpture or just a simple everyday act. The physical form is irrelevant as all the teaching happens at the level of the mind. As such, the form the love takes may not even necessarily be considered beautiful or special in the eyes of the world.

216

Hypnotic Spirituality

Indeed, it may not even have any visual effects. This love just acts as a reminder to others that they too can make a better choice.

With this in mind, we realize that we can all be prophets, at least occasionally and temporarily. The Course says that "Miracles are performed by those that have temporarily more to those who have temporarily less" (miracle principle #8), that is by those who are currently in their right mind to those who are currently in their wrong mind. When in our right mind, we become teachers of God (at least temporarily). We're not teaching on the stage or pulpit, nor are we foretelling the future. Through the love that currently flow through us and the peace that inhabits us, and by seeing shared interests instead of separate interests, teachers of God simply become a reminder to their brothers that they can make the choice for love. This presence of love and peace in us is what helps us "teach" to those who have chosen the wrong thought system, by our demonstrating the right one.

The first step is to accept people as they are and where they are in their spiritual progress. Nobody is inferior or less worthy – just like a 5th-grader is no less worthy than a 6th-grader; they are just at different stages in their learning. Similarly, the teacher of God is just another fragment of the Sonship, no better or worse than any other, just temporarily in a better "state of mind". The teacher of God also realizes that he learns as he teaches, and knows to ask the Holy Spirit to be *his* teacher.

Being a teacher of God involves retaining your inner peace regardless of where you are, with whom you are and whatever happens around you or to you. By acknowledging your Christ nature, you can realize that

217

A new prophet

nothing can deprive you of that inner peace (the "stately calm within" or "quiet center"). In other words, there is no change in that loving feeling in you regardless of what someone else does; whatever they do is indifferent to you. Even an attack or harmful act does not disrupt your peace, as you understand it comes from the "attacker's" fear.

By showing their attack had no effect on your inner peace, you are teaching, at a deep unconscious level, that their choice is faulty and they too can (though they may not be willing or ready for it yet) make the choice for love. In a way, we are using God as a model for our reaction: He did not respond to the tiny mad idea, and similarly, we do not respond to the apparent wrongdoings, as we see them as just a misperception. Once again, it bears reminding that all this happens at the level of the mind, and not necessarily on the level of form. Your behavior in the world might still be "normal", but it will not affect your peace.

A CALL FOR LOVE

The second aspect that we must master as teachers of God is seeing everybody's seeming attack as a call for love, and seeing the shared interest with our brothers. As we know, we are all part of the Sonship and, as such, are perfect and whole. Unfortunately, most do not realize this fact, and fall into the vicious circle of attacks described in Part 1 of this book.

The Course teaches us that everything in the world is either an expression of love or a call for love; to which, either way, our response is love. This is another one of those principles that make sense on paper, but is

Hypnotic Spirituality

difficult to put into practice. The core of the problem is that we see people and the world as real. Working through the exercises described in the Chapter 11 ("Just an Illusion"), will help you come to terms with the unreality of the world. By applying these techniques, you can start seeing "people" not as bodies, but as the Christ within them. Once this is established, you can start to see their actions in a different light. Since they are perfect beings, only capable of love, that means their perceived action can only be due to a misperception of their true nature. The guilt of the (seeming) separation leads to fear of punishment, which leads to attacks. Another way to think about it is that the attack is the result of a perceived sense of lack. Wanting to get back what they think you stole from them, they seek and call for love, not realizing they *are* love.

Faced with an attack, don't let it disrupt your inner peace, otherwise you give it power by reinforcing the mistake – but you can react behaviorally. Do not take it as a personal attack. If you attack the other person back, you are really hurting yourself. Be and act normally – as the world would expect you to – but stay at peace. For instance, if you are physically attacked, you may defend yourself like any normal person would, but don't react in mind and be aware of the unreality of the situation. Your train of thought is "you're making a mistake". It's the same attitude you'd adopt when stopping a child from playing in traffic. You can see everyone as a little child, lost, not knowing how to get home and calling for help. Another good application of this principle is at funerals and in hospitals. Do and say what normal people do and say, but do it with a sense of peace (with an inner smile, because you know nothing has happened).

A new prophet

By seeing all attacks from others as calls for love, you effectively demonstrate you see shared interests (our common goal of awakening from the dream) instead of separate interests. By forgiving your brother for what he has not done, you heal yourself. Once again, it's important to realize we're talking at the level of content (i.e. mind) here, not form. In form, the two people involved in the situation are separate, but the process of realizing our shared interest is in the mind. So, from that point of view, the two people are the same; giving and receiving is the same. By giving guilt (in form of attack), you reinforce it in yourself, but by forgiving, you reinforce love in yourself as well.

IN PRACTICE

This is all well and good in theory, but how do we put that into practice, and how can hypnotherapy help us? It is, of course, unrealistic to expect to be perfectly peaceful all the time. We would not be here if we were.

I believe a measure of our spiritual progress is how long we stay upset. In other words, how long does it take us to forgive and regain our peace. As described in the chapter "Face Lift", it is a lot easier to stay peaceful once you realize that *you* are the cause of all the things that upset you and all the disrupting elements are really projections of your own thoughts.

So, the first part of achieving this peace relies on the approach given earlier, where we installed triggers to catch ourselves when feeling victimized, reverse the projection and see the seeming victimization as a decision we made (refer to the "Face

220

Hypnotic Spirituality

lift" chapter for details). "Catching" yourself is indeed the crucial first step in my opinion, as without awareness of what you are doing, it is impossible to correct it. Once again, the key is to not judge yourself or feel guilty in those cases, but to observe the situation and your reaction to it, and accept that it is a natural part of having a split mind. The law of cause and effect implies that identifying in mind with the Holy Spirit (the thought of love and peace) will naturally yield love and peace.

We can also apply some standard hypnotherapy stress relief techniques, used to provide help in remaining calm. For example, a popular and effective metaphor used to relieve stress is one of a boiler. The boiler represents the tension and stress accumulated in the client. Instead of being an impotent victim of the pressure building in the boiler, the client learns to control the boiler and release steam to regulate the pressure and keep the "machine" running smoothly. This metaphor can be used to control your internal peace by using an "ego" lever and a "Holy Spirit" lever (see Andy's story below for an example).

NLP-inspired techniques can be used to locate a source of anger in the body, describe it and release it by letting it slip out (through the fingers for instance).

I also like to use a technique called "Protective Shield", a metaphor in which clients imagine a sort of bubble around them, that will protect them from negative outside influences, or whatever they want to feel protected from.

1. Induce a state of hypnosis

A new prophet

2. Feel the relaxation spread through your body
3. See that feeling of relaxation extend past your skin to form a sort of bubble around you
4. This bubble acts as your protective shield against anything you want
5. You can use it as a filter against perceived attacks
6. Picture one such attack and see it turn into a call for love as it passes through the bubble
7. Picture a situation that would usually cause you to get upset and see the upset feeling bounce off the bubble
8. You can also symbolically picture the ego in some form or another outside the bubble trying to "get you"
9. See it bounce right off the shield provided by the bubble

Another good metaphor that you can use under hypnosis to help become more aware of your oneness and shared interest is one of a pane of glass, which fell and broke into tiny little pieces. This is symbolic, of course, of the separation, and each piece of glass represents one part of the Sonship (not just humans, but also animals, vegetables, minerals, even energies). In this exercise, you associate with one of these tiny pieces of glass, and replay its breaking from one large pane into a multitude of small fragments.

I usually extend the analogy by describing the pane of glass as a holographic one. As we discussed, holograms have the peculiarity that, when the piece is broken in two, the whole image is still in each piece, albeit a little fainter. You can thus imagine yourself as that broken piece of glass, and be aware of the faint holographic image (of Oneness) that was in the whole pane of glass,

Hypnotic Spirituality

and now is present in each individual piece. Feeling this common thread with all the pieces allows you to see the commonality we all share. You can then continue this exercise by imagining the pieces coming back together one by one, eventually rebuilding the full pane of glass that is its true nature.

Andy's story

I applied the classic stress-relief hypnotherapy techniques discussed above (adapted to include Course-relevant notions) during one of my sessions with Andy, an engineer, who despite being very analytical and scientific, was also very spiritual. He understood the concept of the "stately calm within" and keeping his peace, but had a hard time putting it into practice.

We first went through the protective shield exercise. I had Andy imagine a bright light emanating from his body (symbol of the Christ in him), and forming a translucent but impermeable bubble around him. That bubble, I suggested, was to keep the peace in him protected from outside "attacks". As I knew Andy was a sci-fi and cartoon buff, I used sci-fi analogies to give the metaphor more power. We went through a few scenarios where he would have typically lost his peace, and I had him imagine those outside influences bounce right off the shield or get turned into calls for love as they passed through the bubble.

We, then, went through the boiler analogy, using Andy's engineering background to make the metaphor more real for him. In the variation of the standard boiler method, I had Andy picture a source of upset building in him, raising the pressure of the "engine", but realizing

223

A new prophet

that the source of the upset was himself, and not an outside entity. I had him imagine a valve and a meter. The meter was labeled "ego" on the right side and "Holy Spirit" on the left. He learned that he could control the pressure by turning the valve one way or the other. Turning it to the right rose the pressure pushing the needle on the ego side (a symbol of being in his wrong mind), turning it to the left pushed the needle towards the Holy Spirit side (a symbol of being in his right mind). The result was that Andy was now in control of his upset, and not driven by it. He could decide for the Holy Spirit (by turning the metaphorical lever to the left), thereby reducing the pressure (i.e. retaining his peace).

Finally, we went through the glass pane exercise described above. The combination of these three techniques allowed Andy to feel a better sense of oneness and shared interest with others, which in itself yielded some peace. The bubble and boiler metaphor allowed him to further assert responsibility for his peace, and *choose* the Holy Spirit in order to achieve it.

This type of metaphor, though simple and even childish-sounding on the surface, is exactly what helps build subconscious associations, which will take hold and remain active once out of hypnosis, subconsciously guiding you in the application of these principles in everyday life.

Important Note

As helpful as this type of work is, there may be cases where deeper-rooted anger issues are present. For those, I recommend seeking the assistance of a professional hypnotherapist, in order to clear out the "emotional baggage" (see Chapter 7 for details).

CONCLUSION

Spirituality, as defined by *A Course in Miracles*, is simple but not easy. Indeed, it is based on a few fundamental principles that can quickly be understood intellectually, but are very difficult to apply consistently and truthfully. All our upbringing and education occur in the context of the ego thought system, and the unlearning necessary to recognize our true nature is a tremendous endeavor. The Workbook provides invaluable exercises to help us achieve this. But, letting go of our ego habits and adopting right-minded ones to the point where they become an unconscious choice is a tall order.

This book showed you how using hypnotherapy techniques can help you make those principles easier to absorb and therefore help accelerate your spiritual progress.

As a review, here's a quick summary of the main points we covered. You learned how to use hypnotherapy techniques to:

- Look at the world with honesty, and realize there's nothing to lose by leaving it

Conclusion

- See how deeper levels of hypnosis get us closer to our True nature

- Get a glimpse of heaven with deep hypnosis

- Become aware of the illusion of the world and the unreality of time

- See the world as a school instead of a prison

- Experience the world as a projection

- Become conscious of the victimization game you play and your resistance to change

- Handle the ego with the respect it deserves but, at the same time, does *not* deserve

- See all the "parts" of the world as one, and realize their shared interest

- Become aware you have the power to make a better choice, and understand how to make decisions and ask for help in doing so

- Undo the ego's thought system

- And above all, learn to gently forgive yourself when you do not do any of the above

I hope you found the exercises and techniques presented valuable. Remember that these are just examples. Feel free to create your own self-hypnosis sessions to match your style or specificities.

Do not hesitate to e-mail me your feedback, questions or suggestions at philippe@hypnoticspirituality.com.

I welcome both positive and negative feedback. This book is controversial in many ways. First of all, *A Course in Miracles* (in the non-edulcorated interpretation that I follow) is a radical thought system that, in and of itself, disturbs a lot of people – as it brings into question all that they believe as true. And, hypnotherapy, though more accepted in recent years, still has an aura of suspicion around it. Applying hypnotherapy to Course practice is bound to attract attacks from both Course purists, who will say the Course is complete and does not need any help in applying its principles, and classic therapists who will question the application of professional hypnotherapy techniques to such a "woo-woo" subject as spirituality.

I am thankful for all the upcoming attacks and disparaging comments, which I welcome as a great forgiveness opportunity.

Have fun!

APPENDIX A
-
SAMPLE SCRIPTS

Sample scripts

SAMPLE INDUCTION

The following is a classic progressive relaxation induction which can be used to ease yourself into a gentle state of hypnosis. It works well as a general-purpose induction.

You could record this for your own use during your sessions or have someone read it to you.

The "..." indicate a slight pause.

◆

Sit or lie down in a comfortable position, with your back supported, your hands at your sides and your legs uncrossed.

Let your eyes close gently, and start becoming aware of your breathing... Focus on slowing down the rhythm of your breathing... Feel your abdomen expanding outward with each breath you take, like a balloon filling up with air...

Slowly take a deep breath in... Pause for a moment... and then exhale slowly. And, with every breath you take in, you inhale peace and relaxation... and every time you exhale, you breathe out stress and tension... Let all the tension melt away as you relax more deeply with each breath...

Continue breathing slowly and gently...

Now, turn your attention to the top of your head. Very few people are aware of the tiny muscles of their scalp. So, feel the relaxation beginning at the top of your head,

Hypnotic Spirituality

feeling all those tiny muscles relaxing... then spreading slowly downwards...to your ears... Feel your eyebrows gently resting downward... Your forehead is becoming relaxed and smooth...

Let the relaxation extend to your temples... and your cheeks... your nose... your eyes... Let your jaw relax by allowing your mouth to be gently part and your chin to relax downwards... Allow your tongue to relax...

Your entire face is now totally relaxed and expressionless... and all the little lines of your face are smoothed out...

Continue to enjoy the feeling of relaxation you are experiencing...

Now turn your attention to your neck... allow a feeling of relaxation to begin at the top of your neck, and flow downward...

As you feel the relaxation spreading to your shoulders, and let them gently sink downward... as they become relaxed... and heavy... very heavy... very loose and relaxed... deeper and deeper... relaxed...

Notice your breathing once again... see how smooth and regular it has become... continue to take slow, steady, deep breaths... Breathe in the feeling of relaxation... and breathe out any tension... your breathing allows you to become more and more relaxed... so deeply relaxed...

Sample scripts

Now, turn your attention to your right arm... Feel the relaxation flowing down from your right shoulder... to your upper arm... your lower arm... your wrist... your hand... all the way to the tips of your fingers... the relaxation spreading to your thumb... index finger... middle finger... ring finger... and little finger...

Picture all the tension and stress flowing out through your fingertips...

Enjoy that feeling of relaxation, as all the muscles of your right arm are now loose and limp...

Now, feel the relaxation flow down your left arm... from your left shoulder... to your upper arm... your lower arm... your wrist... your hand... all the way to the tip of your fingers... the relaxation spreading to your thumb... index finger... middle finger... ring finger... and little finger... Picture all the tension and stress flowing out through your fingertips...

Enjoy the feeling of relaxation as the muscles of your left arm are now loose and limp...

Let the feeling of relaxation continue to flow... spreading easily down through your body... spreading to your chest and stomach... feel the relaxation there... becoming looser with every breath... Feel your torso becoming heavy and your body sinking into the surface beneath you...

Now, turn your attention to your upper back... Feel the relaxation flow down your spine... Let all your back muscles become loose... relax your upper... middle... and lower back... allow your back to relax completely...

232

Hypnotic Spirituality

Let the muscles of your hips relax now... Relax all the way from your buttocks... down your thighs... moving down to your knees... your calves... shins... ankles... and feet... allowing all those muscles to relax and go limp...

Allow any last traces of tension to flow out though your feet... Feel the waves of relaxation spreading from the top of your head, drifting through your whole body, to the tip of your toes... becoming more and more relaxed with each breath... enjoying this feeling of total relaxation...

You are now more relaxed than you've ever been before... Enjoy this wonderful feeling if relaxation... calm... and peace that envelops you.

Sample scripts

SAMPLE DEEPENER

The following is a fairly standard deepener that can be used after your induction. The purpose of the deepener (as the name suggests) is to guide you into deeper and more stable states of trance. The "..." indicate a slight pause.

◆

Now that you are so relaxed, you can let your mind wander... and imagine you are standing at the top of a staircase... which leads to a beautiful peaceful garden... the garden of relaxation...

The sun is shining... the sky is blue... the air is warm... and your skin is caressed by the gentlest of breezes... In the distance, you hear the gurgling of water from a stream...

As you look down into the garden, you can see beautiful trees and flowers... and smell their aroma.

There are 10 steps leading down to the garden... and, in a moment, I am going to count from 10 down to 1... and with each number, you will take a step down towards this beautiful garden of relaxation... becoming more and more relaxed with each step...

10...Take your first step down now...feel the peace and calmness envelop you...
9...
8...Becoming more and more relaxed...
7...

Hypnotic Spirituality

6... Deeper and deeper relaxed
5...
4... As you take this step down, you double the relaxation
3... You can now smell the sweet aroma of the flowers in the garden...
2... Almost there now...
1...Deeper and deeper relaxed...
0... You feel a complete sense of peace come over you, as you step onto the soft grass of the garden...

You take a few steps... and admire the beautiful flowers...and listen to the chirping of the birds in the trees...

As you wander deeper and deeper... into the garden, you notice a bench facing a peaceful pond... You walk over to the bench and sit comfortably... enjoying the serenity of this garden of relaxation...

You are now in a deep state of relaxation... more relaxed than you ever thought possible... and in this deep state of relaxation, your mind is now open to accept and absorb new ideas, new concepts and suggestions for positive change, ...

Sample scripts

SAMPLE EMERGING SCRIPT

The following is a standard emerging script that you can use at the end of your session, in order to come out of the state of hypnosis. The "..." indicate a slight pause.

◆

In a moment, I am going to count from 1 up to 5, and on the count of 5, and not before, you will open your eyes and feel fully alert and refreshed...

1... slowly, easily let yourself come back to awareness
2... you feel every nerve, every cell, every fiber of your body totally relaxed...
3... rising slightly more now... becoming a little more aware of your surroundings
4... almost there now... feel the energy returning to your body... you're feeling perfectly rested as if rousing from a pleasant doze...
And 5... all the way up now... fully alert, feeling wonderful in every way... open your eyes and notice how good you feel...

APPENDIX B

RESOURCES

Hypnotic Spirituality

RECOMMENDED READING

A Course in Miracles is obviously required reading. However, it is very radical and easy to misinterpret.

There are also several well-known authors who offer a watered-down interpretation of the Course, which may appeal to those who are not willing to accept yet the full message of the Course. But, I believe it is better to hear the real message of the Course (and acknowledge you are not ready to accept it fully yet), rather than a "feel-good" version of it.

The following books provide what I consider the most honest explanation of the Course principles and I recommend reading them to help make sense of those concepts.

- **The Disappearance of the Universe** by Gary Renard (Hay House Publishing). A very good introduction to the Course, whether you believe the premise of the story or not.

- **Your Immortal Reality** by Gary Renard (Hay House Publishing). A good follow-up to *Disappearance of the Universe*.

- **All books and audio programs from Kenneth Wapnick** (www.facim.org/bookstore/default.aspx). Ken was the main editor of the Course, and his teachings are clear and uncompromising. I am grateful for his work, and I owe most of my understanding of the Course to him.

Resources

- The foundation for a Course in Miracles is also an excellent resource.
  http://www.facim.org/

◆

The following two books, though not placed in the context of the Course, will help you grasp some of the concepts of oneness and our shared interest from a more scientific point of view.

- ***The Holographic Universe*** by Michael Talbot (HarperCollins)

- ***The Field*** by Lynne McTaggart (Element Publishing)

◆

Finally, the following book provides a thorough introduction to self-hypnosis.

- ***Self Hypnosis: A Step-by-step Guide to Improving Your Life*** by Valerie Austin (Thorsons)

There are obviously many more books that could be mentioned, but I've decide to keep things simple so that the readers are not overwhelmed with information.

240

RECOMMENDED MOVIES

- **The Matrix**: this movie will help you wrap your head around the idea that this world is an illusion and a projection. The difference is that, instead of many people attached to the matrix, there is really only One.

- **Avatar**: another useful film to accept that the body we think we are may not be ours, but driven by another mind (the decision maker).

- **Inception**: this film also helps question the reality of the world and the notion of time.

HYPNOTHERAPY WEB SITES

If you are looking for a certified hypnotherapist to help you with your *hypnotic spirituality* (or other hypnotherapy work). I would suggest you seek out the main hypnotherapy association in your country to ensure you find a suitably qualified therapist.

Note that in some places, the term "hypnotherapist" can only legally be used by medical doctors. In those locales, the term "hypnotist" is used by lay practitioners.

Resources

Here are some associations I recommend:

- In the UK:
    o APHP (www.aphp.co.uk)
    o NCH (www.hypnotherapists.org.uk/)
    o GRH (www.general-hypnotherapy-register.com/)

- In the US, the National Guild of Hypnotists (ngh.net)

For Past Life Regression, here are a few helpful links:

- www.iisis.net/index.php?page=semkiw-past-life-regression-providers&hl=en_US
- www.pastliferegression.co.uk/database.htm
- www.earth-association.org/

The above is by no means a complete list of resources. Please refer to your country's hypnotherapy authorities for a more comprehensive list. Also, directory web sites such as those listed above come and go, so please visit my site (www.hypnoticspirituality.com) for an up-to-date list of resources.

Printed in Great Britain
by Amazon